SPAIN

1 SEVILLA. The Alcázar: Patio de las Doncellas (Maidens' Courtyard).

SPAIN

MARTIN HÜRLIMANN

---

237 PICTURES IN PHOTOGRAVURE

8 COLOUR PLATES

INTRODUCTORY ESSAY

AND NOTES

THE STUDIO PUBLICATIONS INC.

in association with

THOMAS Y. CROWELL COMPANY

NEW YORK

II TOLEDO. View of the town across the Tajo from the south.

SPAIN

A PENINSULA in the south of Europe, separated from the rest of the Continent by a high mountain range; a Catholic people with a strong sense of family loyalty, and speaking a Romance tongue; a nation whose claim to world status is still being upheld in art and in literature—this describes both Italy and Spain. But beyond the Pyrenees the northerner will find not only a scenery which differs appreciably from that south of the Alps, and the monuments of a differently conditioned history—he will find that he himself becomes a different being there.

When in Italy, we follow in the footsteps of Byron and Stendhal, of Goethe and a procession of pilgrims that spans the centuries; there we visit the cities of the ancient world, the Holy See, the places where the medieval rulers of the West were crowned; we enter the palaces of the Renaissance princes, where our humanistic civilization flowered most splendidly. We step out of our northern workaday life into a world of light, a holiday world; there we expect to find the lovelier side of the picture.

But Spain represents, even by popular tradition, something strange, foreign and proudly inaccessible. Coming from "la doulce France", with its living comfort and the soft light of its green valleys, another world greets us here: steppes and plains Asian in extent, canyon-like valleys in which we seem to be transported to America, palm-oases nestling between barren wastes reminiscent of North Africa.

A vast, primeval mass of earth, the *Meseta* occupies much of the interior of the very nearly square peninsula. Like bastions the Cantabrian, Iberian and Baetian cordilleras enclose the high plateaux of Old and New Castile, across which bitter winds sweep in winter-time, but on which the sun beats down without shade or pity during the brief summer months. Although Spain has the sea on most of its borders, it is one of the loftiest lands of Europe, and its climate is a continental one. Madrid, the present capital, is situated well over 2,000 feet above sea-level, 220 miles by road from the nearest port (Valencia). Also, the historic centres

7

of culture of Castile and León lie appreciably higher than the principal cities of so mountainous a country as Switzerland: the altitudes of León, Burgos, Salamanca, Segovia, Avila
range between 2,650 and 3,710 feet, whereas those of Geneva and Berne are only 1,234 and
1,780 feet, respectively.

The wide plains are intersected by deep gorges which the rivers have hollowed out and
by rugged mountain ranges, and on the trunk roads, however much they may wind, one
encounters many a steep gradient. Both the Atlantic and the Mediterranean coasts are mostly
steep and rocky; it is only here and there that the coastal belt broadens out into fertile acres
such as the verdant Huertas around Murcia and Valencia, where oranges, figs and dates
thrive. The southerly-flowing Guadalquivir alone, of all the Spanish rivers, runs through a
broad valley of luxuriant cornfields, olive groves and vineyards, which the ancient Romans
and the Arabs developed into one of the most opulent and densely populated regions of
Europe. In the north-east the Ebro divides the Meseta from the Pyrenees and provides a connecting link between Navarra and the Catalan coast, though it is no more navigable than the
other Spanish rivers; however, it guided the aspirations of the kingdom of Aragon towards
the Mediterranean, the Balearics, and beyond to Sicily and Naples.

Spain's rich ore deposits were exploited already by the Iberians and Phoenicians. The
Romans set their slave masses to the task of digging lead, tin, iron, copper, silver and gold,
and thereby met a large part of their empire's financial requirements. Nowadays the once so
important copper and silver mines of Andalusia are of very much less significance than the
coal and iron-ore mines of the Asturian-Cantabrian mountains.

Spain is a big country full of solitude. Its roads still belong to those who ride on muleback,
drowsily perched on the rear end of their pack-animals, and to the wayfarer. As though at sea,
the motorist sails along, often with his vehicle as sole company for hour after hour. Between
the widely separated landmarks of cathedral towers, the turrets of castillos, the villages untouched
by mechanization, he meets with occasional flocks of sheep—sometimes they are goats or
little black pigs—grazing upon the tough grass growing between rocks on the hillsides or
gleaning forsaken fields.

In the North, along the Basque, Asturian and Galician coasts, which are laved by the
Gulf Stream, we encounter, beneath a frequently overcast sky, familiar scenes of green woods
and meadows, where the sturdy inhabitants with their Sunday bagpipe-playing might at
first sight be men of Scotland. Andalusia, which is synonymous with sunshine and the South,
has by virtue of the gypsy and Moorish element in its native music, its pageantry, bull-fights
and castanet dances, supplied the local colour for *Carmen* and many another opera by
Mozart to de Falla.

The great mosque of Córdoba, the gardens of the Alcázar in Seville, the courtyards of the Alhambra in Granada transport us to the world of A Thousand and One Nights. Valencia is the typical white Mediterranean town, instinct with life and energy but dropping into a lengthy siesta at midday; Barcelona is like a chessboard of streets filled with industrious Catalans; while in distant Santiago de Compostela, St James the Greater, pilgrim's staff in hand, has silently received the nation's prayers over a thousand years. The wealth of contrasts knits together into an overall impression of grandeur and austerity.

The highland plateaux of the Meseta, haughty, inaccessible Castile with its castles around which the winds whistle, with its herdsmen who protect themselves from the cold or the heat by wrapping themselves in their *ponchos*, with its patient donkeys and mules—these constitute the kernel of Spain.

*   *   *

The Pyrenean peninsula served already in prehistoric times as a bridge between Europe and Africa: the mysterious rock-paintings of Altamira, dating from many centuries before the Christian era, were the work of a race of hunters, whose like we encounter again in the caves of the Dordogne and in Africa. We attribute Hamitic-North African origins to the so-called Iberians; these mingled with the Celts who advanced across the Pyrenees. During the time that, from the eighth century B.C. onwards, Phoenician traders were founding their "factories" along the Mediterranean coast, the Celtiberians were already developing a civiliza-tion of their own, and had begun to work the Andalusian copper mines. The very earliest records concerning the inhabitants of Spain mention characteristics which will become significant in this country's subsequent history: a sense of honour, bravery, pride; their highly developed individualism, which is coupled with a marked lack of community sense, resists major political alliances, yet is capable of unqualified loyalty towards their elected leader in battle.

Individual Phocæan colonies opened the way for the civilization of the Greeks. Carthage entered upon the legacy of the Phoenicians and took possession of the Strait. The Romans took up arms against its commanders Hamilcar, Hasdrubal and Hannibal. For a few years (227-219 B.C.) it seemed as if the Ebro was destined to become the frontier between the two opposing realms; but before long Rome had only to contend in Spain with the Celtiberians themselves. Nonetheless, it cost the greatest military power of ancient times many heavy losses in battle before it succeeded in gaining control of the entire peninsula. The superior statecraft of the usurpers was ultimately able to ensure victory over the obstinate separatism of races braver than they. Under Augustus even the proud peoples of the Asturian and Basque hill-country were finally subdued.

No other area subject to Rome acquired for her such significance as the Hispanic provinces: the wealth of its fertile acres and its mines became indispensable to the empire, while the creative genius of its people put new blood into the body politic and cultural. The emperors Trajan and Hadrian were born and bred in Spain, the philosopher Seneca and his nephew Lucan came from Córdoba, the poet Martial from Bilbilis in the Celtic uplands, Quintilian from Old Castile and the Emperor Theodosius the Great was born in Coca in A.D. 347.

To no other country, what is more, did Roman rulership bring more lasting foundations for its ensuing life as a nation. On every hand we find traces of Roman military roads, which for the first time made possible a centralized administration; from Mérida to Lumbier, from Salamanca to Tarragona bridges and aqueducts, city walls and triumphal arches are still in evidence. Under the *Pax Romana* Spain got to know the blessings of a central authority, which brought a variegated mixture of races together in reaping the rich harvest of the land. Among the immigrants of this period were the Jews, who were henceforward to play such an important role in Spanish commercial and cultural development, and at the same time that steady flow of people of divers races began, who were bought and sold on the Mediterranean slave markets until fairly modern times.

In the third century, according to Tertullian, Christianity had already spread across all the Hispanic provinces. Two Spaniards, the poet and hymn-writer Prudentius and the historian Orosius, reinterpreted Rome's mission, likening it to a preparation for Christendom, which was to awaken the subject peoples to new life. In the year 325 Bishop Hosius of Córdoba exercised a leading influence at the Council of Nicæa where Athanasius gained his decisive victory over Arianism.

In 409 invading hordes descended with the suddenness of a catastrophe upon the territory on which a weakened empire's grip was relaxing. Vandals, Suevi and Alans swept down from the Pyrenees as far as the south coast, pillaging as they went. Gaiseric removed from Andalusia —whose name recalls the Vandal occupation—to Africa in 428. Under Ataulphus the Visigoths, too, streamed across the Pyrenees in 415; as allies of the Emperor Honorius they captured the Provincia Tarragonensis together with Barcelona, and so began the ascendancy of this East Germanic race which was to last close on three hundred years; gradually their rulers—sometimes as nominal vassals of the Roman Empire, sometimes as its enemies—brought the whole peninsula into subjection.

The Goths brought with them their system of elective kingship, whose power was kept within bounds by virtue of an intrinsic nobility and spirituality. Only commanding personalities were able to keep the disruptive forces of particularism in check. The political maxims and laws of state which underlay Germanic thought merged with the Roman traditions.

III GRANADA. Jardín de Machuca and west front of the Alcázar.

Latin was adopted as the official language. Of still greater significance was to be the victory of Roman Catholicism over Arianism. The Arian Visigoths were tolerant by nature; they did not interfere with the Catholics and also tolerated the Jews. From Andalusia, however, where Roman strongholds were maintained well into the sixth century, the Catholic teaching of Athanasius was energetically fostered, until finally the universal validity of the Apostolic Creed was accepted at the Gothic kings' court: the Third Council of Toledo endorsed the Catholic teaching in 589. The official faith was enforced by law, and so began the compulsory conversions and the expulsions of the Jews.

Under the Visigoths trade and culture enjoyed a fresh period of prosperity comparable to that of the best days of Rome; Archbishop Isidore of Seville, whose renown as a scholar shone for centuries like a beacon in Europe, described Spain at the close of the fifth century as "the finest of all the countries that extend from the Occident to India, blessed and fortunate in its princes, mother of so many peoples".

Thus, under its Germanic kings, Spain appears to have attained national status sooner than any other European country, showing all the characteristic traits with which we have since come to associate her. And yet an occurrence was imminent, which threatened to cut off the Iberian peninsula for ever from the European comity of nations and their civilization.

*

Rivalry for the Crown, the Jewish problem, the covetousness of the nobility, all these had allowed the anarchic forces latent in this country to gain the upper hand once more, and the most powerful race of conquerors of the period did not need much encouragement to enter upon the scene. The empire of the Syrian Arabs under its Caliph was at this time at its zenith and controlled the Mediterranean coast of Africa. In the year 711 Musa, viceroy of the Omayyads, sent his commander Tarik with a Berber army to Andalusia, and himself landed there with fresh troops a year later. The sovereignty of the Caliphs of Damascus was proclaimed in Toledo in 713, and within seven years the Mohammedans had occupied the greater part of the peninsula. Their further thrust into France was thwarted by Charles Martel's victory at Poitiers (732), but in Spain the "Moorish" hegemony was to last for hundreds of years.

The "Moors" were hardly less rent by internal strife than the Christians. To the rivalry of the viceroys and army commanders were added outside influences from Africa and distant Syria. When the Omayyads were overthrown and the caliphate passed to the Abbassids in Baghdad (750), an independent rulership established itself in Spain. A descendant of the Omayyads, Abdurrahman II, who had escaped from the bloodbath of Damascus, was recognized as emir by a concert of notabilities in Córdoba in 756. He had to contend not only with the Christians in the north and east of the country, behind whom stood the power of Charles the Great, but also with the Arabs of North Africa and the Abbassids. The foundations of the new dynasty were, however, solid enough to endure for very nearly three centuries (until 1031). The court of Córdoba became a forcing-ground for the arts and sciences, among which mathematics in particular gained world renown. Christian and Jewish scholars contributed to the city's fame; the learned nun Roswitha in distant Gandersheim described it with wonder as "Ornamentum mundi". Apart from a few fragments in museums there is little to remind us today of the splendour of the rulers' palaces, but the "Mezquita" or Great Mosque, one of the supreme shrines of Islam, still stands; with its hundreds of ancient columns and Visigothic capitals, it remains, even though a cathedral has since been built into it, one of the most magnificent memorials to the Moors in Spain.

The Islamic invasion added to the racial mixture a thin upper stratum of Syrian Arabs and large numbers of African mercenaries and slaves. Nevertheless, the Omayyads brought to the whole country the blessings of a just rulership; they allowed the Spanish tongue to be spoken in addition to the official Arabic, and Christian and Jewish forms of worship were not ousted by the Mohammedan state religion. Abdurrahman III, who in 929 was the first to assume the title of Caliph—Arabic "successor", but adopted to denote "head of all the faithful"—sent Bishop Recemund, a noted astronomer, as envoy to the emperor, Otto I, and to Byzantium and Jerusalem. The Arabs renewed and improved the Roman irrigation systems, they encouraged the cultivation of Oriental fruits and plants, introduced silkworm rearing into Andalusia and brought book-learning to a high pitch through manufacturing paper and building up libraries. Trade and industry benefited by the nimbleness of the Jews. The Spain of the Moors was at this time the wealthiest and the most densely populated land in Europe.

But with the decline of the Omayyad dynasty at the turn of the first millennium anarchy and internal rivalry among petty usurpers once more gained the upper hand. Nor did the campaigns of the terrible El Mansur, a mighty warrior-hero, succeed in preventing the collapse of the autonomous state. The realm of the caliphs broke up into a series of little principalities.

Towards the close of the eleventh century the mighty new Berber empire of the Almoravids struck at the European continent; their Sultan Yusuf assumed the role of defender of Islam against the advancing Christian armies, and the cultivated life of luxury of the peaceable little courts yielded to renewed religious fanaticism. In 1146 there was yet another African invasion of Moorish Spain; this time it was the Almohads, a Berber race from the Atlas. Their rulers chose Seville as their place of residence. This period has bequeathed us the huge minaret tower of the "Giralda" as well as the palace buildings of the Alcázar, which were enlarged

iv SAN SEBASTIÁN. View from Monte Igueldo eastwards across the bay.

in the fourteenth century by the Castilian rulers, particularly Peter the Cruel, though their Moorish character was preserved, Moorish workmen being employed.

The battle of Navas de Tolosa near Jaén in 1212 resulted in a decisive victory for the Christian "Reconquista" over the Mohammedans; yet a remnant of the Almohad empire was able to hold its own for 280 years in Granada, and to this last epoch of Moorish Spain we owe the Alcázar of the Alhambra, whose halls and courtyards with their distinguished contours and extravagant wealth of ornamentation are among the world's wonders of architecture.

*

The demise of the refined, tired civilization of Granada spelled the victorious end of the Reconquista, which for centuries had made Spain the battle-field between Islam and Christianity, Orient and Occident. This struggle, so fateful for the whole of Europe, was by no means waged between entirely self-contained protagonists who were always aware of the fundamental issue. There were great commanders and rulers on both sides, who personified the historic missions upon which they were bent; but there were also disastrous ruptures resulting from personal feuds amongst clans and classes and between usurping chieftains. Centuries of peaceful co-existence would follow upon years of bloody campaigns, and the tension caused by religious fanaticism would ever and anon yield to a desire to reap, in commerce and culture, the harvest of a more tolerant régime. Rivalries and special relationships would lead to alliances and vassal servitude which cut across religious scruples. With the continual ebbing and flowing of battle every change of rulership did not necessarily result in the extermination of those of a different faith, let alone those of a different race; compulsory mass conversions and expulsions were the exception, toleration was the rule. Thus, in the Islamic realm the Christian Arabs or *Mozarabs*, in the Christian states the Mohammedan *Mudéjars* and the converts to Christendom known as the *Moriscos*, all played a significant role.

The Moors never succeeded in completely subjugating the peninsula. In their hiding-place amid the Asturian mountains the fugitive Christians in 718 rallied around Pelayo, a last descendant of the Gothic kings. His successor Fruela founded Oviedo, which became the centre of a kingdom destined to grow steadily in power and influence. A second rallying-point of the resistance was built up in the region of the Pyrenees. Among the smaller sovereign authorities which frequently incorporated French territory, Navarra and Aragon developed into important kingdoms and rivals for the leadership of all Spain. In Barcelona Charles the Great established the "Spanish March", which after the withdrawal of the Franks continued as an independent county, and finally united with Aragon.

Under a succession of energetic rulers Asturia grew into the kingdom of León. The many castles, which were erected particularly in the eastern frontier area, gave this district the name of Castile; it was here that Alfonso III founded the town of Burgos in 882. The severest setback the rising state received was at the hands of the aforementioned El Mansur, whose hordes in 977 laid waste the new pilgrims' mecca of Santiago. Ferdinand I made Burgos the focal point of the united kingdom of Castile, León and Galicia; his armies penetrated far into Moorish territory. Alfonso VI (1072–1109), who assumed power after the assassination of his brother Sancho II, renewed the victorious campaigns of his father Ferdinand and wrested Toledo from the Mohammedans. His title, "Emperor of all Spain, lord of the peoples of both religions", indicates what wide claims were made for his monarchy. A century later Ferdinand the Holy, conqueror of Córdoba, went so far as to call himself "King over three religions", whereby he acknowledged the Jews in addition to the Christians and Moors in his kingdom. In Toledo there is a magnificent synagogue, built in the style of a mosque, which recalls this magnanimous attitude of the Christian conquerors; this rare edifice was able to survive the periods of relentless religious persecution which later ensued only by virtue of being converted into a church (Santa María la Blanca). Time and again the monarchs had to take into their protection the peoples of another faith with whom they were entrusted, and whom they needed to develop the country. To offset the covetousness of the nobility the Crown relied upon the industrious population of the towns; already at an early date the organization of the "Cortes" assured the citizenry of a considerable voice in the country's affairs.

The reign of Alfonso VI represents the zenith of the Spanish heroic age, which, glorified by the poets, has assumed an almost legendary air. During the campaigns of the Reconquista was born that type of warrior and overbearing individual who was later to become the conquistador of the New World. The ideal of the knight without fear or blame was most wholly personified in one, Rodrigo Diaz, whom the Moors admiringly called the Cid, that is, the Master. Exiled from Castile, he laid the foundations of his renown in the service of the Moorish ruler of Saragossa, before placing himself once more at the disposal of his king; it was in Valencia, which he conquered twice, that he ultimately wielded absolute power.

The existence of Portugal as a separate state can also be traced back to the time of Alfonso VI; for in 1095 the king of Castile transferred to his son-in-law Henry of Burgundy the newly constituted province which could rely on the support of the Pope and, later, the alliance with England in developing into an independent kingdom.

James I (1213–76), known as "the Conqueror", meant to the kingdom of Aragon what Alfonso VI meant to Castile: in Catalonia and along the Mediterranean coast one often encounters traces of him; he occupied Valencia and the Balearic Isles, helped Ferdinand III of Castile to conquer Seville, and his dominion extended well into France.

As the Christian realms broadened, the conquerors were faced with numerous colonizational problems. Among the most active pioneers were the monastic Orders. Situated in lonely mountain valleys, the fortified monasteries of the Benedictines, Cluniacs, Cistercians and Hieronymites remain as impressive landmarks of the Reconquista. The faith took possession of a virgin country; it brought the colourful mixture of races its unifying message. There were miracles and supernatural occurrences, while the fame of certain wonder-making images drew pilgrims from far and near; in particular, the tomb of the Apostle James in Galicia gave rise to a ceaseless pilgrimage from the direction of the Pyrenees through the Christian kingdoms of northern Spain.

Out of neighbouring France, on the heels of the monks and pilgrims, came master-builders and artists. In Catalonia many a portal and cloister recalls the Romanesque churches and monasteries of Provence. Burgundian influences spread farther west; in Galicia we encounter the Toulouse School, and, as opposed to the few surviving monuments from the days of the Visigoths, which might have given rise to a national style, the example of the French cathedrals became predominant. Amongst this preponderance of foreign designs and from out the anonymity of the architects and sculptors, one indigent master stands out in solitary greatness, at the threshold of the Gothic period: on the "Pórtico de la Gloria" of Santiago, where James the Greater with his pilgrim's staff sits enthroned amid a concourse of prophets and apostles beneath a picture of the Redeemer, to receive the faithful, the name Mateo and the year 1183 are engraved. The equals of Santiago in the grand scale of their conception and the wealth of their ornamentation are the mighty cathedrals of Burgos, León and Toledo. In these monuments of Castilian dominion over the entire Meseta northern French Gothic achieved a triumphant flowering also on Spanish soil. In 1402 work was begun on a dome above the mosque in Seville; it was to serve as a symbol of the conquest of Andalusia, and those responsible meant it to exceed in splendour all others of its kind. Other influences besides the French made themselves felt in the fifteenth century: the Ebro valley turned towards Italy, Castile adopted countless artists from the Netherlands, while in Burgos Hans of Cologne and his son erected the twin-towered cathedral front.

*

Under Ferdinand and Isabella, who have gone down in history as the *Catholic Monarchs*, Spain entered the ranks of the world powers as a unified nation; the very union of this exceptional couple derived from its functioning as a sovereign entity. Called to the throne of Castile as the sequel to a confusion of events, the eighteen-year-old Isabella chose for husband, from among numerous suitors and against the wishes of her royal brother Henry IV, the Crown Prince of Aragon, who was a year younger than herself; disguised as a groom, Ferdinand reached Valladolid after an adventurous journey, and there the couple took the law into their own hands and were wed on 19 October, 1469.

In 1479 Ferdinand II embarked upon sole rulership over his hereditary Aragonese possessions. He attacked the forces of separatism with the patient determination of the born statesman; he mastered the art of intrigue-ridden diplomacy as have few other crowned heads. Purposefully he pursued the traditional policy of Aragon towards France, particularly in the Mediterranean, and at his death Roussillon, Sicily, Sardinia and half Italy were united under his Crown. In the person of Isabella the serpentine cunning of the politician was coupled with the devout soul of a visionary who believed implicitly in the divine right of kings. There was an irrational streak in the genius of this woman, who was the daughter of a madwoman and herself gave birth to a mad daughter.

The insubordinate nobility bowed to the combined wills of the Catholic Monarchs, the roads became safer, trade flourished. Whereas the royal couple's two realms were still ruled separately and various traditional rights and privileges were respected by the strengthening monarchy, the sovereigns founded the unity of the nation primarily upon the unity of the Catholic faith. To keep this faith uncontaminated and strong, above all among the many newly converted Moors and Jews, was the task of the Inquisition, which was introduced under papal authority in 1480 and was organized on a nation-wide scale.

The supremacy of Castile caused Castilian to be used increasingly as the language of the realm and it became the organ of a rich national literature. Thanks to her close ties with Italy, Spain participated actively in the flowering of Humanism. The universities, pre-eminently the already world-renowned Salamanca, strove to introduce universality into thought, and the devout Cardinal Cisneros, who had succeeded the noted politician Mendoza as Archbishop of Toledo and adviser to the monarchs, founded a centre for Bible research and linguistics in Alcalá de Henares. In architecture also, catholicity of outlook led to a national synthesis. Now, too, the Moorish forms of the south began to blend with foreign elements, among which Isabella herself favoured the Flemish, and this resulted in a new Spanish style. In addition to splendid churches and chapels, arose palaces and college buildings whose porticoes and patios were richly carved and ornamented.

On 2 January, 1492, after ten years of warfare, the Moorish kingdom of Granada capitulated. Upon the capture of this last bulwark of Islam, whose conquest Isabella in

v VALLADOLID. The Caritas Procession.

particular had striven for with passionate zeal, the Catholic Monarchs treated the beaten enemy with great magnanimity; yet here, too, the Church ultimately introduced a relentless inquisition. On 12 October of the same year Columbus set foot upon a new world and planted the banner of the Catholic Monarchs on American soil. The knights and religious fanatics of the Reconquista were thereby presented with a new opportunity to carry out an historic mission, and they grasped it with both hands.

*

When in 1516 the seventeen-year-old Charles I entered upon his grandparents' heritage in Castile and Aragon as king of all Spain, he arrived as a foreigner surrounded by Flemish advisers. What with the demands of the Cortes and the rebellions of the Communeros, as well as the "Germania" movement with its anarchic tendencies, which originated in Valencia, the reality of the situation in Spain was brought home to him very forcibly. But with mounting knowledge of their language he, too, grew closer to his new peoples and accustomed himself to the difficult art of ruling. His election as emperor, by virtue of which he succeeded his paternal grandfather Maximilian I and assumed the title Charles V, laid further heavy burdens upon the shoulders of the Habsburg heir. Titian, in his superb pictures now in the Prado, has bequeathed us a life-like portrait of this engaging personality, who succeeded in adapting himself to the exacting demands of emperorship. The sincerity of Charles's religious faith enabled him, what is more, to combat the temporal aspirations of the Pope, without wavering in his obedience to the Church and its spiritual leader. The pride and dignity of Spanish deportment pervaded the emperor's court and made Spanish etiquette the model for all Europe.

With the rapid building up of the overseas possessions the knights and missionaries of the Reconquista had found a limitless new field for their activities; riches flowed into the country, and Spain became the leading maritime power. In those buildings which are adorned with the imperial coat of arms the influence of the Italian Renaissance has superseded French Gothic; yet the overall effect is still determined by the "plateresque" ornamentation of doorways or in the detail of the church interiors with their sumptuous, often richly gilded choir screens and retables, and ornate tombs. In his vast retable for San Benito el Real, which, dismantled into its component parts, is still to be seen and admired in the Valladolid museum, Alonso Beruguete gave vent to all the power of expression of a Michelangelo, and so initiated the era of Spanish Baroque. But during the reign of Charles V the Spanish people fulfilled their mission most zealously by playing such a leading role in the so-called Counter-Reformation. The Humanism of Erasmus had found enthusiastic support among scholars who included the highest dignitaries of the Church; but the Inquisition operated more and more stringently and, in its anti-Lutheran persecution, did not stop short of arraigning the Archbishop of Toledo. The conversion of the Mudéjars, whom, particularly in Aragon, their aristocratic employers sought to protect, was enforced in breach of solemn promises, and before long the Moriscos (converted Moors) were also being persecuted. The Church was at this time extending its mission from home lands to overseas territories, while the monarchy was coming to depend more than ever upon a unity of faith. Catholicism in Spain was still abounding in unexpended energy. Visionaries such as St Ignatius of Loyola and St Teresa of Avila had no need of the provocation of Wittenberg and Geneva in order to fire the entire Roman Church with the ardour of their faith.

Charles V was concerned above all to keep the forces of Christianity intact. Within the Occident, whose foremost crown he wore, he strove for peace and mutual understanding, the better to match the Cross against the Half Moon. His son Philip II, to whom the emperor, on retreating to the seclusion of the Yuste monastery in 1556, passed on the Crown of Spain, had no longer to worry about Protestant subject peoples within the realm. He knew only one, indivisible Church, over whose purity the Inquisition kept unceasing watch.

To this day people are divided in their verdict on the lonely figure of the second Habsburg to occupy the Spanish throne. One school of thought regards him as an intolerant autocrat, who revelled in the grim ceremonial of *auto-da-fé*, who obstinately meddled in every detail of state administration while unable to prevent the basic structure of his authority from being whittled away, and who at his death—an anguished one—bequeathed an undermined realm to incompetent successors. For the others Philip—"our great Philip", as Miguel de Unamuno calls him—represented the apotheosis of Spanish dominion, one who, saintlike, withstood every blow of destiny and transcended every human weakness through obedience to the Faith. Philip commissioned his two most able architects, Juan Bautista de Toledo and his pupil Juan de Herrera, to build him a ruler's abode, which uniquely expresses the Spanish idea of kingship: a mighty castle of the Faith, in which, beside the monastery of the Hieronymites and beside the domed church in whose crypt his imperial father, he himself and all his successors shall be laid to rest, the tireless crowned worker has his modest habitation.

*

For a century after the death of Philip II (1598) there were Habsburg rulers, none of whom were capable of arresting the ensuing political decline. But Spanish culture flourished in the seventeenth century as if only now, following the heroic deeds of preceding generations,

the artistic genius of this people had come to fruition. Baroque architecture created a frame of frigid splendour. Colourful and gilded carved figures were carried in procession out of the churches into the streets so that the people should behold in all their realistic pathos the Passion of Our Lord, the Grief and Transfiguration of the Holy Virgin and the enraptured features of the Saints. It was a generation of unrivalled painters, however, who gave most moving expression to the spirit of the time: Ribera, Zurbarán, Murillo and the princely Velasquez disclose beneath the courtly etiquette and the surface pomp the profound melancholy of aristocratic and mature minds. Spanish writers, too, moulded the language to shape its greatest works of literature: the poems of Góngora, the plays of Calderón and Lope de Vega, and pre-eminently the immortal *Don Quixote* of Cervantes. The Spaniard, whose proverbial pride would normally seem to discountenance humour, has a particularly soft spot for the last-named work. In it he sees every facet of his own individualism, from the rough peasant craftiness of Sancho Panza to the haughty otherworldliness of the knight of the doleful countenance which strays amongst the clouds.

*

We deemed it most necessary, in an introduction to this pictorial volume, to mention some of the factors which went to the making of Spain as a nation and which the traveller will encounter there on every hand. We do not feel called upon to deal with all the complex historical developments of more recent times. Hence, we confine ourselves to remarking that under the Bourbons the state on the French pattern (*l'état*) supplanted the ideas of monarchy which had evolved from the Reconquista. The new royal palaces, in particular the great palace in Madrid, became symbols of the centrally administered state. Nevertheless, the separatist and anarchic forces which, no less than the monastic, go to make up the Spaniard's character, received a fresh impetus during the industrial age. Seen in this light the last Civil War, too, with all its heroic conflicting loyalties, appears to us to represent the struggle of two elemental forces in human nature, which we may perhaps call liberty and faith, or individualism and authority. Both concern every Spaniard far more deeply than is outwardly suggested by the ideologies which outside participants superimposed upon them; it is these attributes, too, which carry within themselves the seeds of healing and the promise of a new beginning.

*   *   *

Those who travel in Spain, and venture outside the sphere of the planned tour, are likely to enjoy a hospitality which still preserves much of the Spaniard's hereditary integrity. The handclasp of the innkeeper or the friendly clap on the shoulder convey even to the foreigner with the merest smattering of Spanish that he is welcome as an individual. On each successive journey one notices less of that reserve which invests not only grandees and officials with an air of seeming arrogance, but to which the man in the street tends to resort in an effort to shield his private affairs from prying outsiders.

Three separate journeys, during which I covered several thousands of miles, left me with unforgettable impressions of the landscape's austere vastness and of the monuments from two millennia of power and faith; but I derived my intensest pleasure from contacts with a people of mixed lineage who are united by a pride in individuality. May the ensuing pages engender in those who scan them something of these emotions! I recall with gratitude that road-attendant on a lonely pass, who used the carefully preserved water in an earthenware jar to fill the radiator of my overheated car. And the peasant Esequiel Torego in the Castilian highlands, who insisted that the handsome span of oxen drawing his hand-plough should not merely be photographed, but taken from the best angle and thereby done full justice. And to the Guadalupe monastery, where we were served with a Sunday dinner of many courses accompanied by aromatic vino tinto. I recall the young lorry-driver who helped me to mend a puncture in Lérida, and who, when by a remarkable coincidence a year later and in practically the same spot he collided with my car, had the damage repaired under his insurance policy without a moment's argument. And I think back with pleasure to the repair shop where this work was carried out with almost miraculous speed, the men working day and night, as though it were a matter of life and death to all concerned. Only once did I encounter a piece of downright unfriendliness; it was in the mining district of Asturia, where some road-menders blocked my way; but a Spaniard who was driving behind me came up to me when next I stopped in order to apologize for his fellow-countrymen. Should I not mention, too, the Monsignore in Burgos Cathedral who allowed the visitor to take photographs in the sacred precincts with a gesture of welcome and a smile of goodwill, or, when a procession was in progress in Valladolid, the women all ready lined up and the hooded men who helpfully directed me to the best vantage-points, without thereby in the least detracting from the solemnity of the occasion? These and many other experiences bind the traveller for ever to this proud country in a spirit of regard, friendship and gratitude.

*

The plates in this volume are arranged to correspond to a journey which, beginning at the foot of the Pyrenees at their western end, encompasses the country and finishes back at the

20

VII GERONA. The old quarter and the cathedral.

French frontier in the north-east. From San Sebastian we start off along the border mountains and wind through the Ebro Valley to Saragossa, the capital of Aragon; then return by way of Navarra back to the Biscay coast, which we follow through the Cantabrian Mountains, more or less on the old pilgrim route to Santiago. From Galicia we penetrate to the heart of the Meseta via the ancient kingdom of León, reaching Old Castile with its evocative castles and towns. Next, we traverse the passes of the Sierra de Guadarrama on our way to the highland plateau of New Castile, where lies Madrid, the capital, and Toledo. We visit sundry places of interest in the Mancha and the famous Guadalupe monastery, and pass through the mountain scenery of Estremadura southwards to Mérida, the most important centre of Roman Spain. In Andalusia we admire the residences of the caliphs and kings and tarry awhile in the Oriental fairy-tale world of the Alhambra at Granada. From there we keep to the Mediterranean coast, reaching the frontier territory of the Pyrenees once more in Catalonia.

VIII The MESETA DE LA MUELA, between Zaragoza and Calatayud.

COSTA CANTÁBRICA

ANTUARIO DE SAN IGNACIO DE LOYOLA

LOS ARCOS

ESTELLA

PAMPLONA

PAISAJE CERCA DE JACA

JACA, CATEDRAL

ANTANO DE ARGUIS

PUERTO DE ARGUIS

PAISAJE EN EL VALLE DEL RÍO ARAGÓN

HUESCA. ALTAR MAYOR DE LA CATEDRAL

VIÑEDO EN LA RIOJA, CERCA DE LOGROÑO

VITORIA

PANCORBO

PUERTO DE ORDUÑA

VALLE DEL RUDRÓN

BILBAO

32

SANTILLANA

NTILLANA

RGOS. CASA DEL CORDÓN

CATEDRAL DE BURGOS

CATEDRAL DE BURGOS. PUERTA DEL SARMENTAL

CATEDRAL DE BURGOS   38

CATEDRAL DE BURGOS. SEPULCRO DEL OBISPO MAURICIO   39

BURGOS. ARCO DE SANTA MARÍA

VIEDO, CATEDRAL

42

ALDEA EN ASTURIAS

LLANES

NDOÑEDO

LA CORUÑA

CORUÑA. TORRE DE HÉRCULES

CORUÑA, PUERTO

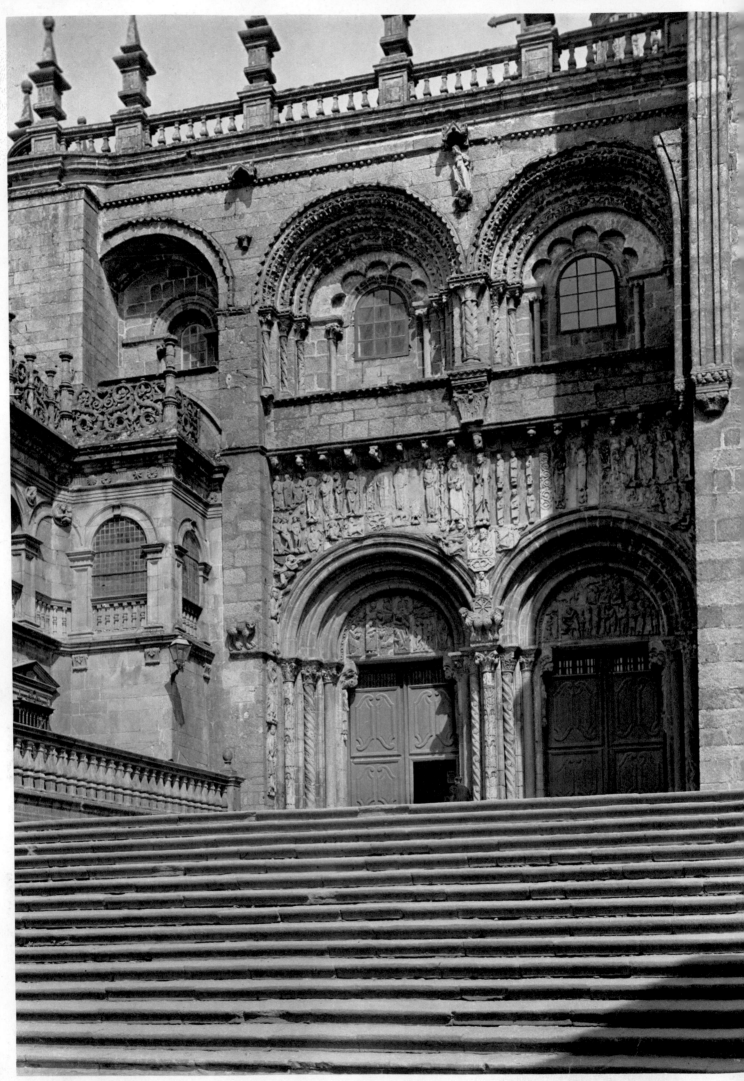

SANTIAGO DE COMPOSTELA, CATEDRAL. PUERTA DE LAS PLATERÍAS

SANTIAGO DE COMPOSTELA, CATEDRAL

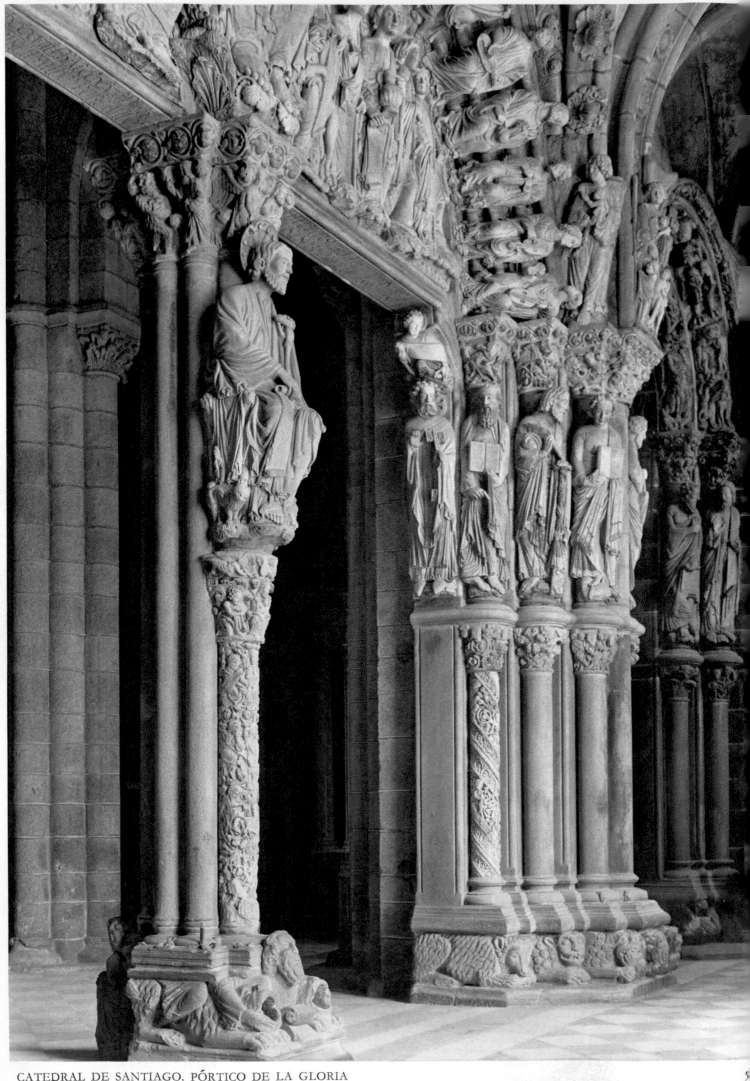

CATEDRAL DE SANTIAGO. PÓRTICO DE LA GLORIA

SANTIAGO DE COMPOSTELA. HOSPITAL REAL

PUERTO DE PIEFDRAFITA

FERIA DE GANADO EN ASTORGA

ÓN. CATEDRAL, CAPILLA DE SANTIAGO

CATEDRAL DE LEÓN

CATEDRAL DE LEÓN. PÓRTICO DE NUESTRA SEÑORA LA BLANCA

LEÓN. MONASTERIO DE SAN MARCOS 61

LEÓN. AYUNTAMIENTO 62

AMORA

BÉJAR

SALAMANCA. SAN ESTEBAN

AMANCA. ESCUELAS MENORES

LAMANCA. PUENTE ROMANO

SALAMANCA. PALACIO DE MONTERREY

LAMANCA. CASA DE LAS CONCHAS, PATIO

SALAMANCA. TORRE DEL CLAVERO

VALLE DEL DUERO

ANDA DE DUERO. IGLESIA DE SANTA MARÍA

MEDINA DEL CAMPO. CASTILLO DE LA MOTA

TORDESILLAS

ÑAFIEL, CASTILLO

DUEÑAS

VENTA DE BAÑOS. BASÍLICA DE SAN JUAN BAUTISTA

TURÉGANO

CANAL DE CASTILLA

VALLADOLID. SEMANA SANTA

85-86

VALLADOLID. COLEGIO DE SAN GREGORIO

LLADOLID. SAN PABLO

VALLADOLID. COLEGIO DE SAN GREGORIO, PATIO

BERRUGUETE: RETABLO MAYOR DE SAN BENITO EL REAL (VALLADOLID, MUSEO)

COCA, CASTILLO

COCA, CASTILLO

ALDEA SEGOVIANA

YUNTA DE BUEYES EN EL CAMPO CASTELLANO

PASTOR EN LAS CERCANÍAS DE SEGOVIA

SEGOVIA. ACUEDUCTO ROMANO

SEGOVIA. ACUEDUCTO ROMANO

SEGOVIA, CATEDRAL

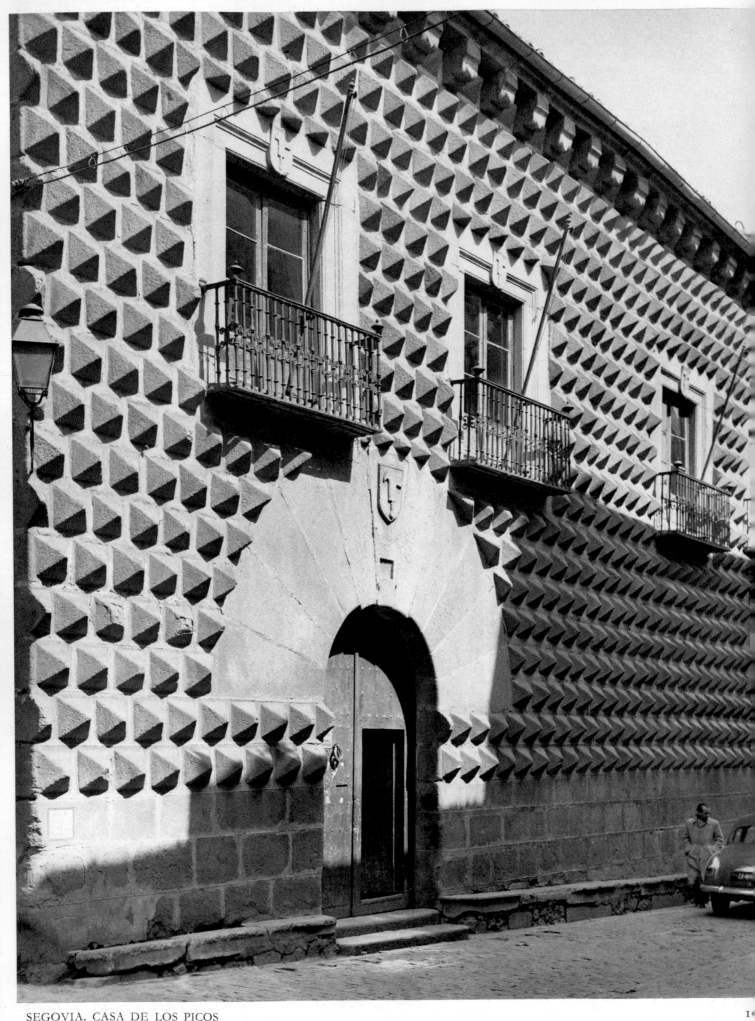

SEGOVIA. CASA DE LOS PICOS

E CAMINO HACIA VILLACASTÍN

VILA

ÁVILA. PUERTA DE SAN VICENTE

ÁVILA. PUERTA DEL ALCÁZAR

ÁVILA. ÁBSIDE DE LA CATEDRAL

ILA. CATEDRAL

ÁVILA. IGLESIA DE SAN VICENTE

JARDINES DE LA GRANJA

LA GRANJA. PALACIO REAL

MONASTERIO DE SAN LORENZO DEL ESCORIAL

SAN LORENZO DEL ESCORIAL. LA ALBERCA

SAN LORENZO DEL ESCORIAL. PATIO DE LOS REYES

MEDINACELI. ARCO ROMANO

I

CATEDRAL DE SIGÜENZA. SEPULCRO DE DON MARTÍN VÁZQUEZ DE ARCE

SIGÜENZA. CASTILLO

GUADALAJARA. PALACIO DEL INFANTADO

ᴸCALÀ DE HENARES. UNIVERSIDAD

ᴸCALÁ DE HENARES. UNIVERSIDAD, PATIO DE PEDRO DE LA COTERA

TOLEDO. PUERTA DEL SOL

OLEDO. PUENTE DE SAN MARTÍN

OLEDO. MURALLAS DE LA CAVA

TOLEDO. CATEDRAL

OLEDO. SANTA MARÍA LA BLANCA

TOLEDO. CASA DEL GRECO

TOLEDO. CASA DEL GRECO

MADRID Y EL PALACIO REAL

MADRID. MUSEO DEL PRADO

ARANJUEZ. JARDÍN DEL PALACIO REAL

I.

RANJUEZ. PALACIO REAL

RANJUEZ. CASA DEL LABRADOR

CUENCA. CASAS COLGADAS

JENCA. CIUDAD ENCANTADA 150

LIVARES ENTRE QUINTANAR DE LA ORDEN Y ARANJUEZ 151

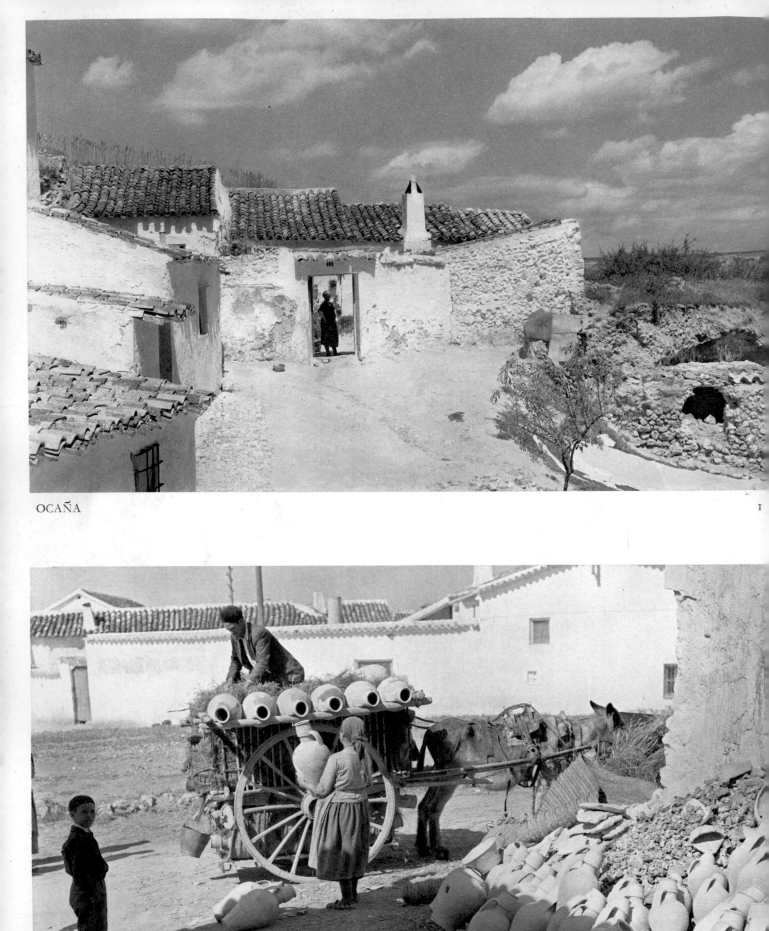

OCAÑA   I

MOTA DEL CUERVO   I

CORRAL DE ALMAGUER

EN UN LUGAR DE LA MANCHA

LAGARTERA

157

OROPESA·

GUADALUPE

GUADALUPE

UADALUPE. CLAUSTRO DEL MONASTERIO

POR TIERRAS DE EXTRAMADURA

PAISAJE EXTREMEÑO

PUENTE DE ALCONÉTAR, SOBRE EL TAJO

TRUJILLO. CASA DEL MARQUÉS DE LA CONQUISTA

UJILLO. ESTÁTUA DE PIZARRO

REVADERO DE CABALLOS EN TIERRA EXTREMEÑA

CÁCERES. CASA DE LOS GOLFINES

SEVILLA

SEVILLA. EL ALCÁZAR

SEVILLA. LA GIRALDA

SEVILLA. CASA DE PILATOS

«SEVILLANA», DANZA ANDALUZA

RONDA

ALDEA DE LA QUINTANA

LOJA

JESTRA SEÑORA DE LA CABEZA

MALAGA

PUENTE ROMANO SOBRE EL SALADO DE PORCUNA

CÓRDOBA. PUENTE ROMANO 18(

CÓRDOBA. PLAZA DEL POTRO 187

CÓRDOBA. CASTILLO DE LA CALAHORRA

CÓRDOBA. LA MEZQUITA

CÓRDOBA. LA MEZQUITA

GRANADA. LA ALHAMBRA

GRANADA. SIERRA NEVADA

GRANADA. ALHAMBRA, MIRADOR DE DARAXA

RANADA. ALHAMBRA, SALA DE LAS DOS HERMANAS

GRANADA. ALHAMBRA, PATIO DE LOS LEONES Y SALA DE LOS REYES

GRANADA. ALHAMBRA, PATIO DE LOS LEONES

198

GRANADA, GENERALIFE

AISAJE CERCA DE MOTRIL

A COSTA MEDITERRÁNEA ENTRE MOTRIL Y ALMERÍA

PAISAJE CERCA DE HUÉRCAL OVERA

ORIHUELA

MURCIA, CATEDRAL, CAPILLA DE LOS VÉLEZ

PEÑÓN DE IFACH

ALICANTE

PALMERAS DE ELCHE

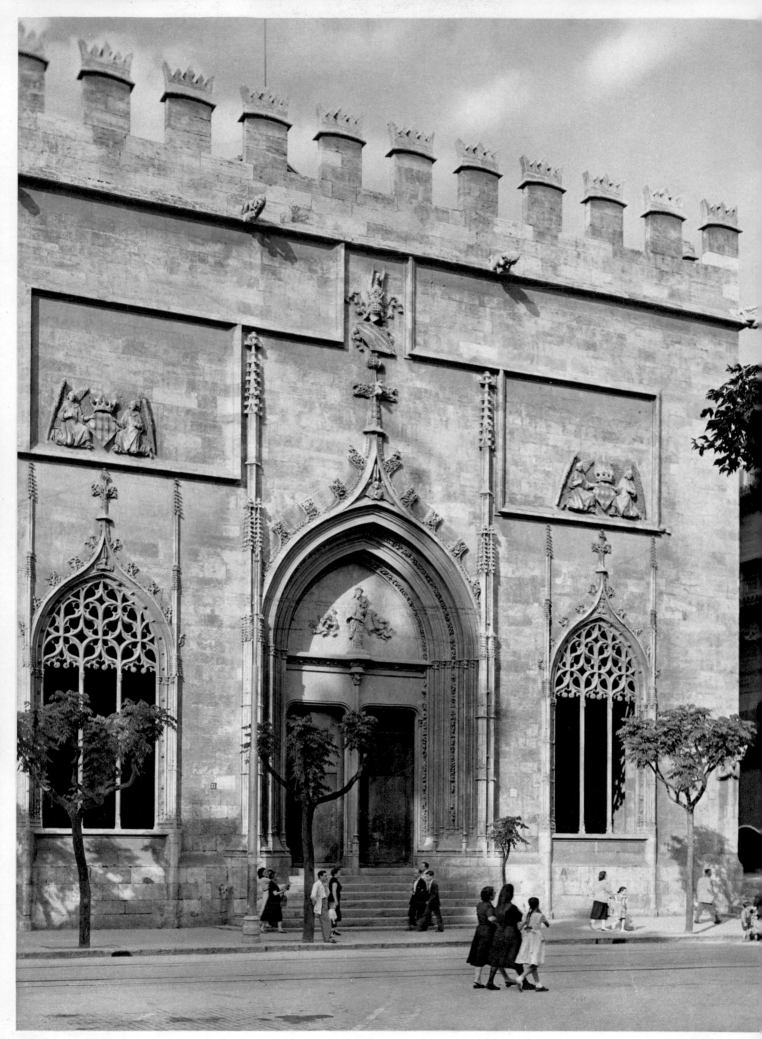

VALENCIA, LONJA

SAGUNTO   212

VALENCIA. TORRES DE SERRANOS   213

PEÑÍSCOLA

REBAÑO DE CABRAS EN LAS CERCANÍAS DE SAGUNTO

TARRAGONA, CATEDRAL

TARRAGONA. MURALLAS ROMANAS

MONASTERIO DE POBLET, CLAUSTRO

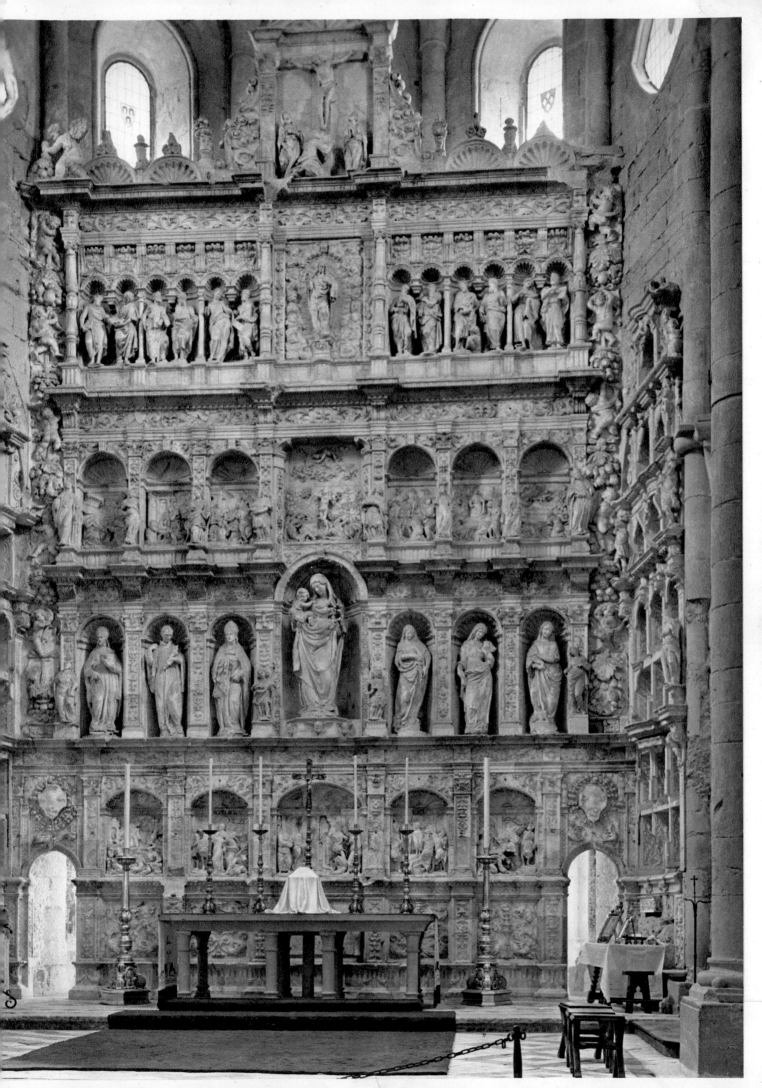

MONASTERIO DE POBLET. IGLESIA, ALTAR MAYOR

PAISAJE EN LAS CERCANÍAS DE IGUALADA

COLL DE NARGÓ

RIPOLL. MONASTERIO DE SANTA MARÍA, CLAUSTRO

RIPOLL. MONASTERIO DE SANTA MARÍA, IGLESIA

VICH. CATEDRAL, CLAUSTRO

ANDORRA. SANTA COLOMA

SEO DE URGEL

MONISTROL

MONTSERRAT. EL MONASTERIO

SITGES

PAISAJE CERCA DE PINEDA

SAN POL DE MAR

BARCELONA. BARRIO GÓTICO

BARCELONA. PALACIO DE LA GENERALIDAD

REPRODUCCIÓN DE LA CARABELA 'SANTA MARÍA', DE COLÓN. PUERTO DE BARCELONA

NOTES ON THE PLATES

Colour Plates

I SEVILLA: The Alcázar. Azulejos (coloured, glazed fayence panels on walls) in the PATIO DE LAS DONCELLAS (Maidens' Courtyard). (*See also* Notes 170–175.)

II TOLEDO. View of the town across the Tajo from the south, with the ruins of the Alcázar forming the highest point; this sumptuous palace, in the building of which Herrera, among others, participated, lost its characteristic silhouette during the shelling of 1936. (*See also* Notes 127–134.) IT IS BEING REBUILT (DONE BY EARLY '62)

III GRANADA. View from the Alcazaba fortress of the JARDÍN DE MACHUCA and the west front of the Alcázar with the great TORRE DE COMARES. (*See also* Notes 192–199.)

IV SAN SEBASTIÁN (Basque: Donostia), capital of the Basque province of Guipúzcoa, lies where the River Urumea flows into the Gulf of Vizcaya. With its numerous luxury hotels, it is one of the world's most fashionable coastal resorts, where during the summer season the country's ministers of state mingle with the aristocracy of Madrid. The population rose to more than 100,000 after the second World War. This town, which went to Castile in about 1200, owes its popularity to its unique situation amid the foothills of the Pyrenees and the Cantabrian Mountains. Our picture shows the view from Monte Igueldo eastwards across the bay (La Concha) with the little island of Santa Clara, the bathing beach and the old harbour, towards Monte Urgull on which stands the Mota Citadel.

V VALLADOLID. The Caritas Procession. (*See also* Notes 83–90.)

VI SALAMANCA. View of the cathedral (sixteenth to eighteenth centuries) from the north bank of the Río Tormes. (*See also* Notes 65–72.)

VII GERONA, provincial capital with a population of 30,000, was the Roman *Gerunda*. It became a bishopric as early as 247. Situated near the Pyrenean frontier, it has, since medieval times, been frequently involved in battles with the French. The old quarter rises steeply up to the cathedral from the banks of the tributary Oñar which, just beyond, flows into the Ter. THERE IS A FABULOUS CLARET

VIII Between Zaragoza and Calatayud lies the Sierra or MESETA (plateau) DE LA MUELA, whose reddish earth is clothed in springtime with flowering broom.

Photogravure Plates

1–2 The CANTABRIAN COAST on the Gulf of Vizcaya between Ondarroa and San Sebastián. Thanks to the mild and humid climate the upper slopes and the steep shores are wooded with pines, eucalyptus, oaks and chestnuts.

3 The fishing village of ORIO on the Cantabrian coast, with its well-protected inner harbour.

4 ONDARROA, a small port on the Gulf of Vizcaya, with slightly more than 6,000 inhabitants. The multi-storied houses of this old place are built in characteristic Basque style.

5 LIZARZA, a Basque village near Tolosa, at the northern approach to the Betelu Pass.

6 Homesteads near Alsasua, built in the characteristic style of NAVARRA province.

7 The Monastery of SAN IGNACIO DE LOYOLA, near Azpeitia, surrounds the "Santa Casa", where on 31 May (or 1 June), 1491, the founder of the Jesuit Order was born. Queen Anna Maria of Austria, widow of Philip IV, inherited the old family seat in 1681 and presented it to the Jesuits; at their behest, eight years later, the Ticinese architect Carlo Fontana started work on the Baroque domed church. In the foreground stands the statue of St Ignatius, who died in 1556 and was canonized in 1622. The Santuario, which was confiscated by Charles III in the eighteenth century, is now in possession of Guipúzcoa province.

8 The little town of LOS ARCOS in the Odrón Valley, dominated by the Church of the Ascension, is surrounded by olive groves.

9–10 ESTELLA, a small town of 7,300 inhabitants on the Río Ega, is of Roman origin. Several Romanesque churches and the ruins of the Santo Domingo monastery recall its palmy days in medieval times, when the kings of Navarra resided here. During the nineteenth century this place served as a stronghold for the Carlists (supporters of the Pretender, Don Carlos, who was proclaimed king in Estella in 1833).

11 PAMPLONA, capital of the province of Navarra, with a population of 46,000, stands on the left bank of the Río Arga, its medieval cathedral silhouetted against the sky. The founding of the city is attributed to Pompey, after whom it no doubt derived its earlier name "Pompaelo". In the early Middle Ages the Visigoths, Franks and Moors fought for this Basque town, until the kingdom of Navarra was founded here in 905. During the siege of Pamplona by the king of Navarra, who in 1521 was trying to wrest his capital city from the French, Ignatius of Loyola received the wound which was so fatefully to influence his future career.

12 ESCÓ, on the Río Aragón between Jaca and Pamplona.

13 LUMBIER. Excavations of the Roman buildings of *Ilumberri*, looking towards the Foz de Lumbier gorge formed by the Río Irati, a tributary of the Río Aragón.

14 The eroded countryside near JACA, on the road to Pamplona.

15 JACA, a town of barely 8,000 inhabitants, was fortified already in early Roman times; it earned particular renown through its successful defence against the Arabs, who in the eighth century had established themselves in near-by Huesca. The cathedral of the eleventh-century bishopric is believed to be the oldest in Spain. A portico with statues dating from the seventeenth century leads to the Romanesque main doorway.

16 The ARGUIS DAM (nearly 4,000 feet above sea-level), on the south side of the Puerto de Arguis, dams the Río Isuela above Huesca. To develop irrigation in this water-starved country must be considered one of the most urgent requirements of present-day Spain. Taken at the end of August, our photograph of the almost empty reservoir emphasizes the importance during a dry summer of safeguarding every drop of water.

17 Lonely farmstead on the PUERTO DE ARGUIS, the 3,280-feet-high pass connecting Jaca with Huesca.

18 Eroded countryside by the RÍO ARAGÓN near Jaca.

19-20 HUESCA, capital town of the province of that name, with a population of 17,500, is referred to by Roman historians as *Osca*. The Arabs took possession of the place in the eighth century, and it was not until 1096 that Pedro I of Aragon succeeded in wresting it from them and re-establishing the bishopric. For the next twenty-two years Huesca was the capital of the kingdom. During the Civil War, from 1936 to 1938, it was one of the most effective strongholds of the Nationalist forces.

The present-day cathedral was built between 1497 and 1515 to the designs of Juan de Ológaza; the main doorway with its many statues was taken from the earlier building (early fourteenth century). Above the High Altar rises a magnificent sixteenth-century alabaster retable.

21 ZARAGOZA (Saragossa), with its 260,000 inhabitants, is one of the leading Spanish cities, containing an archiepiscopal see and a university. The Salduba of the Iberians was developed by Augustus into a military colony and named *Caesaraugusta*, which the Moors called "Saragusta" during their occupation of it from 712 until 1118. After its conquest by Alfonso I, Zaragoza became the capital city of the kingdom of Aragon.

The aerial photograph shows the Old Town on the right bank of the Ebro; near the old bridge, which dates back to the Romans, are the town's two principal churches: right, the cathedral "la Seo", built between 1119 and 1550 in place of a mosque which itself had occupied the site of an earlier church; left, the great Pilgrim Church "Nuestra Señora del Pilar", begun in 1681 to the designs of Herrera.

22 LOS MONEGROS: From the road which climbs between Lérida and Zaragoza views are to be obtained of a broad, desert-like mountain landscape which is sparsely covered with vegetation in the spring.

23 The town of CALATAYUD (Zaragoza province), population about 20,000, situated on the Jalón at 1,740 feet above sea-level, was called *Bilbilis* in Roman times and

was the home town of the poet Martial. The place was rebuilt under the Moors, who called it Qal 'at Ayyūb (castle of the Ayyūb); after it had been recaptured by the Christians, the kings of Aragon and Castile fought for possession of it.

24 The district around Logroño called "LA RIOJA", in the fertile Ebro valley, is noted for its vineyards (red and white grapes). Logroño, the old Castilian capital of the province, is one of the centres of the Spanish wine trade.

25–26 VITORIA, capital of Álava province, population 52,000, 1,736 feet above sea-level, is believed to have been founded by the Visigoths. The former Gazteiz received its present name from Sancho VI (the Wise) of Navarra, who conquered it in 1181; in 1332 the fortified town came into the possession of the kingdom of Castile. It was to celebrate the victory which Wellington won near Vitoria in 1813 over King Joseph and the French that Beethoven composed his "battle Symphony".
The Old Town is situated on the height known as the Campillo. Plate 25 shows the glassed-in balconies (Miradores) in the Calle San Francisco, which are characteristic of the place. The cathedral of Santa María, shown on Plate 26, was built in the fourteenth century. The spacious portico with its three doorways, covered with a wealth of carving, was added during the following century.

27 PANCORBO is picturesquely situated by the gorge which the Río Vallarta has cut for itself through the Montes Obarenes, before flowing into the Ebro at Miranda de Ebro.

28 The BAY OF GUERNICA, at whose southern end lies the little town made famous by a grim event during the Civil War. The winding road which follows the mostly sheer Cantabrian coastline has here to make a detour of several miles inland.

29 View across the green slopes of the Cantabrian coastal hills towards the harbour of the fishing village of Bermeo and the sea.

30 View from the heights of the Oruña Pass (2,950 feet) which traverses the Cantabrian Mountains around the limestone cliffs of the Peña de Orduña, northwards across the valley of the Nervión.

31 The road from Burgos to Santander follows for a time the valley of the Rudrón which has made a deep cleft in the plateau.

32 BILBAO, with a population of some 200,000, is one of the busiest industrial ports in Spain. Factories, docks and wharves extend along the seven and a half miles of the lower Nervión between the town centre and the sea. Bilbao, founded in 1300, did not assume importance until the end of the nineteenth century, when the rich iron mines of the Vizcaya (especially Somorrostro) were developed, aided by the leading finance institutes. Vizcaya province, of which Bilbao is the capital, is the most densely populated area in Spain.

33–34 The little town of SANTILLANA DEL MAR (Santander province), in the vicinity of the prehistoric grottoes of Altamira, grew up around the sixth-century monastery of Santa Juliana (Illana). The main street presents an old-fashioned overall appearance with its houses of the sixteenth, seventeenth and eighteenth centuries, bearing the coats of arms of its noble families.

35–41 BURGOS, principal town of the province of that name, whose population numbers about 60,000, lies on the right bank of the Arlanzón, 2,800 feet above sea-level. Towards the end of the ninth century King Alfonso III of León had a citadel built at this strategically important spot. Once the seat of dukes and kings, Burgos experienced its heyday under Ferdinand I (the Great), who in the eleventh century brought the kingdoms of Castile, León and Galicia under one rule. The Spanish national hero Rodrigo Diaz de Vivar, called the Cid, was born in Burgos in 1026. Alfonso VI, who founded the Roman-hierarchic Church system in Spain, transferred the bishopric of Gamonal to Burgos in 1100; since 1574 it has been an archbishopric. The city lost in importance when the king transferred his residence to Valladolid at the close of the fifteenth century. During the Civil War (1936–9), until the fall of Madrid, Burgos was the headquarters of the Franco régime.

35 On the north side of the Plaza de Calvo Sotelo stands the CASA DEL CORDÓN (named after the cord which is depicted above the coat of arms on the doorway),

the castle-like palace of the Condestable Hernández de Velasco and his wife, Doña Mencia de Mendoza. To the left of the picture a dwelling-house with the characteristic "Miradores" (*see* Note 25) is to be seen.

36-40 The CATHEDRAL OF SANTA MARÍA is one of the most magnificent memorials to medieval Christian times; its exterior recalls the Gothic architecture of France and the Rhineland, whilst its elaborate interior is entirely Spanish in character. The west front (36), whose lower portion lost its Gothic sculptural ornamentation in the eighteenth century, is surmounted by two 275-feet-high spires, which were built by Hans of Cologne in the middle of the fifteenth. On the south side steps lead up to the Puerto del Sarmental, built in the French style in the thirteenth century (37). The central tower was begun in 1466 by Hans of Cologne; its sumptuous interior (38) is attributed to Philip of Burgundy, whose assistants completed the detail in 1567. The choir contains the tomb of Bishop Mauricio, an Englishman who, with Ferdinand III of Castile, founded the cathedral in 1221, and died in 1238; his enamelled copper effigy was produced in Limoges (39). The choir screen, typical of the decoration of Spanish cathedrals, dates from 1602 (40).

41 The ARCO DE SANTA MARÍA, through which the town is entered from the south, was erected in 1536 in honour of Charles V. Beneath the statue of the Archangel Michael the emperor is depicted surrounded by famous characters of the heroic age: to the left of him Fernán González, to his right the Cid, and in the bottom row Nuño Rasura, Diego Porcellos and Laín Calvo.

42 OVIEDO, today a provincial capital with a university and 50,000 inhabitants, was in the ninth century the principal town of Asturia; as such it took a leading part in the Christian resistance against the Arab invasion. In 762 Fruela founded the first basilica here; the present cathedral arose between 1388 and 1528, and is a leading example of Spanish Late Gothic; the 260-feet-high tower dates from the final period. Both town and cathedral were badly damaged during the revolt of 1934 and at the beginning of the Civil War.

43 Farm and granary in Asturia.

44 LLANES, an old port in Asturia (Oviedo province), owes its importance to the iron and copper mines inland.

45 The Cathedral Square of the little Galician town of Mondoñedo (Lugo province).

46-48 LA CORUÑA (Corunna), beautifully situated on a peninsula, is the principal town of Galicia. With a population of 100,000, it is one of the busiest and most elegant commercial centres of Spain. The large natural harbour had already attracted the Phoenicians; the Romans developed the place, particularly under Trajan. Its early origins are evidenced by the so-called "Tower of Hercules" (47), a lighthouse, parts of which date back to the first century B.C., and may even have originated with the Phoenicians.
The town was occupied by the Visigoths, and by the Arabs; in the eleventh century it belonged to the kingdom of Galicia, and in the fourteenth fell to Portugal before being finally taken over by León-Castile. In more recent times it served as a naval base in the wars against England; the port received a severe setback when Spain's Central American possessions were lost in her war against the United States.
Plate 48 shows the inner harbour (Dársena), along which runs the Avenida de la Marina (46) with its arcades and the housefronts completely encrusted with "Miradores" (*see* Note 25), which have earned La Coruña the name "City of Crystal".

49-53 SANTIAGO DE COMPOSTELA owes its renown as one of the three most important medieval Christian places of pilgrimage—the others were Rome and the Holy Land—to the legend of the miraculous discovery there of the tomb of the Apostle James (St James the Greater) in the ninth century. From the direction of the Pyrenees the pilgrim bands journeyed by way of Estella, Burgos, León and Ponferrada into Galicia. The Apostle James became the national hero of the Spaniards, who, using "Santiago" as their watchword, plunged into the battle to drive out the infidel. Up to the time of its capture and pillage by El Mansur, the place had been called Iria Flavia; it was only after its recapture that it was given its present name by Pope Urban II. In 1075 work was started, under Alfonso VI, on the great CATHEDRAL (Plates 49-52), which was built above the old ninth-century burial church; the Romanesque south porch "Puerta de las Platerías", with its wealth of sculptural ornamentation recalling the Toulouse School, dates from this period. The west front (50), one of the most splendid examples of

Spanish Late Baroque (known as "Churriguerism" after José Churriguera), was begun in 1738 by Fernando Casas y Novoa, who died a year before its completion in 1749. Behind this façade stands the PORTICO DE LA GLORIA (51–52) bearing the date 1183 and attributed to the Master Mateo, who was head of the Masons' Guild from 1168. The many figures in the three porches serve to render them jointly the most lavish legacy by way of medieval sculpture on Spanish soil. In the centre, above a column with a relief showing the Tree of Jesse, the Apostle James with his pilgrim's staff can be seen (52); on either side, figures of prophets and apostles.

53 One of the handsomest buildings among the churches, monasteries, palaces and colleges which surround the cathedral is the HOSPITAL REAL, founded by the Catholic Monarchs; the sumptuous porch is the work of Enrique de Egas, who built it in 1501–11.

54 LUGO, provincial capital and bishopric with a population of 21,000, situated 1,525 feet above sea-level, is one of the oldest towns in Galicia; the name "Lug" is of Celtic origin. Under Augustus *Lucus Augusti* became the seat of a "conventus juridicus". The city walls with their fifty round towers (Cubos) were erected by the Romans in the third century.

55 PONFERRADA (León province) is situated 1,780 feet above sea-level at the confluence of the Sil and Boeza rivers. Known to the Romans as *Interamnium Flavium*, it became in medieval times an important stage on the pilgrim route to Santiago. The town is dominated by the twelfth-century Templar castle.

56 The PUERTO DE PIEDRAFITA, 3,640 feet high, lies on the frontier between Galicia and León. The stone-built farmsteads bordering the pass road are characteristic of this mountainous district.

57 Cattle market in León province.

58–62 LEÓN, capital of the province of that name, with a population of 44,000, is situated 2,700 feet above sea-level on a fertile plateau. It was once the headquarters of the Roman *Legio Septima Gemina*, who lost it to the Goths in 540, who in turn yielded it up to the Moors; but it was retaken in 742. In 910, when the realm of Alfonso III of Asturia was split up, León became the capital of an independent kingdom, which had to

contend with fresh Arab invasions and went to Castile in the eleventh century.

The cathedral of SANTA MARÍA DE REGLA (58–60) was founded in 1205, and is predominantly thirteenth-century, owing much of its Gothic quality to the cathedrals of northern France (Rheims, Chartres).

58 The Capilla de Santiago at the north-east end of the choir, with its tall Late Gothic windows, dates from the fourteenth century.

59 View of the south side, showing one of the two towers of the west front.

60 The central porch of the west front, with statue of the Mother and Child on the central support.

61 The monastery of SAN MARCOS at the north-east end of the town was founded in 1513 by Ferdinand the Catholic to replace an earlier lodging-place for the Santiago pilgrims. It was built under Charles V, between 1537 and 1549, to the designs of Juan de Badajoz in the ornate plateresque Spanish Renaissance style.

62 Patio of the Ayuntamiento (Town Hall), erected by Juan Rivero in 1585.

63 ZAMORA, provincial capital, with a population of 32,000, is situated 2,100 feet up on the right bank of the Duero. From the seventh century onwards it assumed considerable strategic importance during the clashes between the Arabs and Christians; in the eleventh century Ferdinand I helped it to recover from the various invasions. The lines, "Back, back, Don Rodrigo! Back, back, proud Cid!" remind us of the fruitless siege of Zamora on the part of the Cid, who together with Sancho II sought to capture the town from Doña Urraca, Ferdinand's puppet ruler. Our picture shows a view of the town from the south bank of the Duero across the old stone bridge with its fifteen arches. In the background to the left can be seen the cathedral, largest of the four Romanesque churches dating from the twelfth century.

64 BÉJAR (Salamanca province), a small town where cloth is manufactured, lies at the foot of the Gredos Mountains, 3,000 feet above sea-level.

65–72 SALAMANCA, capital of the province of that name, is situated 2,625 feet above sea-level, and has a population of about 72,000. Named "Route of the Orient and

207

Princess of the Occident" by Rafael Laínez Alcalá, Salamanca is, by virtue of its wealth of historical buildings and its still flourishing intellectual life, one of Spain's leading cities. Originally established by the Ligurians, *Salamantica* was occupied by Hannibal in 217 B.C.; the Romans made it a stage-point on the Via Lata from Mérida to Zaragoza; in the sixth century the Vandals came upon the scene, followed by the Visigoths; in the seventh century the place came under Moorish rule, and remained so until Alfonso VI won it for Castile in 1085. Under Alfonso IX of León the first college was established in 1218, while in 1254 Alfonso X (the Wise) of Castile gave its first constitution to the newly founded university. Salamanca soon became, particularly during the fifteenth and sixteenth centuries, a centre of culture. Latter-day personalities such as Miguel de Unamuno, its rector of long standing, have lent added lustre to Spain's foremost university.

65 The main gateway of the old UNIVERSITY BUILDING is ornamented with an elaborate bas-relief in the plateresque style of the early sixteenth century: the central medallion at the bottom contains the likenesses of the Catholic Monarchs; above this, the coat of arms of Charles V; at the top, the Pope.

66 The church of SAN ESTEBAN or SANTO DOMINGO is a Gothic building with a plateresque façade, erected by the Dominicans between 1524 and 1610 to the designs of Juan de Álava.

67 Patio of the so-called ESCUELAS MENORES, built in the sixteenth century.

68 This bridge over the Tormes, a quarter of a mile long with twenty-six arches, dates back to the days of Trajan and Hadrian, but was reconstructed in the fifteenth and seventeenth centuries.

69 The PALACIO DE MONTERREY, built in 1540 to the designs of Juan Gil de Hontañón. The most aristocratic Spanish families used to provide their sons with a palace in Salamanca where they could live while they were studying there.

70 Patio of the CASA DE LAS CONCHAS, one of the finest examples of Spanish architecture in the time of the Catholic Monarchs (late fifteenth century).

71 TORRE DEL CLAVERO, built at the end of the fifteenth century by Francisco Sotomayor, the "Clavero"—that is, Keeper of the Keys—to the Order of Alcántara.

72 Associated with the CATEDRAL NUEVA, the city's chief landmark (*see* colour plate VI) is the CATEDRAL VIEJA, a Romanesque building of the twelfth century. An overwhelming sense of vastness is conveyed by this view up into the central dome (Torre del Gallo).

73 The DUERO in the Castilian uplands between Peñafiel and Valladolid.

74 The church of Santa Maria in ARANDA DE DUERO, a town in Burgos province, is a foundation of the Catholic Monarchs dating from the end of the fifteenth century. The elaborate façade is attributed to Simon of Cologne, son of Hans of Cologne, and his successor in the erection of Burgos Cathedral.

75 The CASTILLO DE LA MOTA in MEDINA DEL CAMPO (Valladolid province) was built for King John II in 1440 and used by the Court of Castile. Cesare Borgia was imprisoned in the fort; Isabella, one of the Catholic Monarchs, died here in 1504, and her daughter Johanna the Mad occupied the watch-tower during the last year of her life.

76 TORDESILLAS, a little town on the Duero in Valladolid province, was a residence of the kings of Castile and won renown by virtue of the agreement which the Catholic Monarchs here concluded with Portugal on 7 June, 1494, through the mediation of Pope Alexander VI, concerning the distribution of the newly discovered overseas territories.

77 On a rocky prominence above PEÑAFIEL on the Duero stands one of those massive castles which gave the land of Castile its name. Sancho García was responsible for the original building of the eleventh century; it was then reconstructed in 1307 by Juan Manuel.

78 DUEÑAS is situated on a height overlooking the plain through which the Castile Canal and the Pisuerga flow.

79–80 VENTA DE BAÑOS, in the "Tierra de Campos" of Palencia province, was already used by the Romans as a bathing resort. The remains of a temple to the Goddess of the Thermae were used when the Basilica of SAN JUAN BAUTISTA was erected in the reign of King Receswinth (661). The triple-aisled church is one of the best preserved monuments from the time of the Visigoths after their acceptance of the Catholic faith.

81 Beyond the wide market square of the little town of TURÉGANO (Segovia province) rises the fifteenth-century Castillo. It incorporates the thirteenth-century church of San Miguel, and is one of the most imposing castles of Old Castile.

82 The CASTILE CANAL was constructed between 1753 and 1832 to transport the corn grown on the uplands of Castile; it connects Valladolid with Álar del Rey, and its total length, including the Campos Canal, is over 360 miles.

83–90 VALLADOLID, a provincial capital with a population of 124,000 and situated 2,483 feet above sea-level, has been a university town since 1346 and a bishopric since 1495 (becoming an archbishopric in 1857). Its name derives from "Balad Walid"—the territory of the Walid—in the days of Arab rule. From the thirteenth century on, it became the favourite place of residence of the Castilian kings, until Madrid was finally made the capital of Spain at the beginning of the seventeenth century. During the thirteenth and fourteenth centuries the Cortes met here ten times. The town took part in the rising of the "Comuneros" against Charles V, who preferred to exercise his Spanish rule from Toledo. Valladolid's most important buildings date from the heyday of Castilian artistic achievement in the fifteenth and sixteenth centuries, whilst the museum in the former Colegio de San Gregorio contains by far the most noteworthy collection of Spanish Renaissance and Baroque sculpture.

83 PIETÁ, a polychrome wood carving by Gregorio Hernandez (or Fernandez), who hailed from Galicia but worked from 1605 until his death in 1636 mainly in Valladolid. The group is typical of the "Pasos" which today still are borne through the streets of the town during the nocturnal Good Friday procession.

84–86 Photographs of the Caritas Procession held on Maundy Thursday, which is one of the climaxes of the "Semana Santa" in Valladolid. The celebrations during Easter Week in the old capital of Castile are distinguished by their singularly dignified ceremonial and the splendour of the countless "Pasos" with their representations of the Passion. The members of the lay

groups (Cofradias) who bear the Pasos during the processions are attired in distinctive coloured clothing which usually includes a pointed cowl completely concealing the face.

87 The COLEGIO DE SAN GREGORIO was built in 1488–96, in the reign of Isabella the Catholic; the plateresque façade is attributed to Enrique de Egas.

88 The façade of the church of SAN PABLO. It was Cardinal Torquemada, father confessor of Queen Isabella, who in 1463 had it redecorated in the ornate plateresque style so characteristic of Spanish Late Gothic.

89 Patio of the COLEGIO DE SAN GREGORIO (see 87).

90 "The Conversion of Totila", a wood relief in polychrome lavishly gilded, from the enormous Retablo (altar reredos) which Alonso Berreguete carved in 1529–32 for the monastery church of San Benito el Real. Now in the San Gregorio Museum.

91–93 The CASTLE OF COCA (Segovia province), one of the most magnificent in Castile, was the residence of the house of Fonseca (now in possession of the Alba family). This mighty Moorish-Gothic building was erected in about 1400 for Alonso de Fonseca, Archbishop of Seville.

94 Village in the CAMPOS CARPETANOS near Segovia.

95 Peasant ploughing in the Campos Carpetanos.

96 A flock of sheep grazing in the vicinity of Segovia.

97–102 SEGOVIA, provincial capital with a population of 24,000, is situated 3,300 feet above sea-level on a rocky incline in the valley of the Río Eresma. Until 80 B.C. the Celtic Iberians defended the place against the Romans, who subsequently rebuilt it. For two hundred years it was an Arab city of consequence; later, under the medieval Christian kings, Segovia continued to be one of the chief capitals in the land, where the Castilian Cortes frequently met and Isabella the Catholic was proclaimed queen in 1474.

97–98 The ROMAN AQUEDUCT, probably built under Trajan during the first century, is a masterpiece of early architecture; it consists of granite blocks without cement. The supply channel carries the waters of the Rio Frio ten and a half miles from the Sierra de Fuenfria into the town. The aqueduct itself, which runs through the present-day suburbs, is 890 yards long and has 128 arches; these, where they cross the street, are 95 feet high.

99 On the site of the cathedral, which was destroyed in 1520 during the rising of the "Comuneros", Juan Gil de Hontañón and his son Rodrigo erected the present one in 1521–77. With its 360-feet-high tower, which dominates the town, it ranks as a leading example of Spanish Late Gothic.

100 The sixteenth-century CASA DE LOS PICOS was originally a part of the town's fortifications and served as the official residence of the mayor, who used to receive the king here and obtain his oath to respect the town's privileges.

101 The Romanesque church of SAN MILLÁN was built in 1200 on the south-eastern edge of the town.

102 The ALCÁZAR soars above the confluence of the rivers Eresma and Clamores. In the eleventh century the Caliph of Córdoba had a fort built here, which Alfonso VI of León later extended on the pattern of the Alcázar in Toledo; it was still further enlarged by some of his successors. The bulk of the present-day building dates from the restoration following the disastrous fire of 1862; it houses the Spanish military archives.

103 On the road between Segovia and Villacastín, with the snow-covered peaks of the Sierra de Guadarrama in the background.

104–10 ÁVILA, provincial capital with 20,000 inhabitants, lies 3,560 feet above sea-level. As the place where St Teresa (Teresa de Jesus) was born and active, it became a vigorous centre of the Counter-Reformation in the sixteenth century. The first church of the Roman *Avela* is said to have been founded as early as the year 65 by St Segundo, a companion of St Peter the Apostle. The church of San Vincente commemorates the martyrdom of the saint of that name at the beginning of the fourth century. From the eighth to the eleventh century the town was occupied by the Arabs; the battles which led to its recapture by the Christians number among the most popular topics of the Reconquista saga. The atmosphere of chivalry which surrounded Ávila, oft-times the place of residence of the

minority kings, is indicated by the appellation "de los caballeros".

104 View from the CUATRO POSTES across the Old Town, which is still wholly enclosed within the square formed by the twelfth-century walls. These mighty fortifications, part of which are Roman, are just under a mile and a half in length. The 40-feet-high wall is buttressed by eighty-eight towers made of granite blocks. The cathedral occupies the highest point; in the north-west corner (outside the walls) is the San Segundo chapel.

105 The SAN VINCENTE GATEWAY, at the northern end of the east wall.

106 The ALCÁZAR GATEWAY, at the southern end of the east wall, the busiest of the town's eight gateways.

107 Looking along the north wall.

108 Built into the eastern side of the city walls is the fortified apse (Cimorro) of the cathedral.

109 The CATHEDRAL OF SAN SALVADOR, constructed of grey granite of the district, was begun in the middle of the twelfth century. The view from the Early Gothic aisle towards the Romanesque apse is, as in most Spanish cathedrals, interrupted by a screen decorated with reliefs dating from the sixteenth century and a marble crucifix.

110 Statue group representing the Annunciation in the doorway of the church of SAN VINCENTE (twelfth century).

111 The MONASTERY OF EL PAULAR, the earliest in Castile, was founded in 1390 by Henry II in a valley at the southern foot of the Sierra de Guadarrama. The present structure dates mainly from Baroque times.

112 The CASTILLO DE MANZANARES EL REAL was built in the fifteenth century by Juan Guas for the Mendozas, a noble family whose members distinguished themselves by their services to the royal house of Castile.

113–14 The NAVACERRADA PASS, rising to over 6,000 feet, traverses the pine-clad heights of the Sierra de Guadarrama.

115–16 LA GRANJA (i.e. "the dairy-farm") or SAN ILDEFONSO derives from the hermitage which Henry IV had built for himself here in the woods on the northern slopes of the Guadarrama Mountains, 3,900 feet above sea-level. Subsequently, the Bourbon King Philip V, taken by the situation of the place and its cool climate, chose it as a site for a summer residence patterned upon Versailles: the palace, designed by Teodoro Ardemans, was erected between 1821 and 1823, while two French-men, René Carlier and E. Boutelon, laid out a park with a wealth of statues and ornamental waters.

117-20 The Real Monasterio de San Lorenzo del ESCORIAL is the singular creation of Philip II. After the Battle of St Quentin, fought against the French on 10 August, 1557, he vowed to build a monastery dedicated to St Lawrence, whose feast day it was. In April 1563, at a spot some thirty miles from Madrid, on the southern slopes of the Guadarrama Mountains over (3,000 feet above sea-level), was laid the foundation stone of the great edifice which should serve as a memorial to his Catholic Majesty and in which the ornate plateresque style of the Renaissance period was replaced by the severe classical Spanish Early Baroque. Juan Bautista de Toledo was responsible for the designs; after his death in 1567 his favourite pupil Juan de Herrera completed the work. The ground-plan of the whole is intended to represent the grid-iron on which St Lawrence was martyred. In addition to the granite-like stone of the district, known as "berroqueña", which determines the overall effect, valuable materials were brought from different parts of Europe and from America. The whole complex of buildings, which is 676 feet long by 528 feet broad, with sixteen courtyards, was completed in September 1584; it included a monastery for the Hieronymites, an offshoot from Guadalupe, in addition to the king's residence. In the crypt beneath the dome of the church the Emperor Charles V, Philip II and their successors on the Spanish throne lie buried.

117 View of the Escorial from the vantage point (Silla del Rey) where Philip used to sit upon one of the rocks and watch the building work proceed.

118 The Escorial seen from the north.

119 The southern frontage, with the wing which still serves as a monastery.

120 The Courtyard of the Kings (Patio de los Reyes), showing the church front; the six huge statues of the kings of Judah are by Juan Bautista Monegro.

121 MEDINACELI (Soria province), whose heights (3,330 feet above sea-level) dominate the deeply indented valley of the Río Jalón and the Zaragoza-Madrid road, was once a Roman strongpoint; the stone arch dates from the second or third century.

122-3 SIGÜENZA (Guadalajara province), 3,245 feet above sea-level, is today a little town of 4,600 inhabitants. In former times it was a stronghold of the Celtiberians in their battle against the Romans in 195 B.C.; became a Roman fortification; was destroyed by the Vandals in the fifth century; was made a bishopric under the Visigoths; was occupied by the Arabs in the eighth century, and won back by the Christians in the twelfth. In 1936-7, during the Civil War, it was the scene of heavy fighting.

122 In the CATHEDRAL is the tomb of Don Martin Vazquez de Arce, known as "Doncel", who fell in 1486 while fighting the Moors. It is a masterpiece of Spanish Renaissance sculpture.

123 The CASTILLO, also known as the Alcázar, was built in the twelfth century and reconstructed during the fourteenth and fifteenth.

124 GUADALAJARA, provincial capital with a population of 23,000 and situated 2,228 feet above sea-level, derives its name from the Arab Wād al-Hiğāra, meaning "stone river"; it was conquered in 1085 by one of the Cid's companions on behalf of Castile. The poet Iñigo López de Mendoza, marqués de Santillana, duque del Infantado, died here in 1458. His descendants were responsible for the creation, from 1461 onwards, of the magnificent PALACE OF THE DUKES DEL INFANTADO, designed by Juan Guas. The French king Francis I was housed here tem-porarily after his capture at Pavia, and it was the scene of the wedding of Philip II and Isabella of Valois. The famous courtyard was destroyed in 1936 during the Civil War, the west front alone being left intact.

125-6 ALCALÁ DE HENARES, a settlement already in Iberian, became known as *Complutum* in Roman times. A bishopric under the Goths, it became an Arab fort—al-Qal'a—to which, together with its situation on the River Henares, it owes its present name. It was recap-tured by the Christians in 1118. In 1510, Cardinal

Jiménez de Cisneros, who as Archbishop of Toledo was ruler of the town and who numbers among the leading figures of the Spanish Church, founded the world-renowned UNIVERSITY here. In its heyday in the sixteenth century it could boast 12,000 students, most of whom came to study languages. Cisneros was instrumental in the compilation between 1514 and 1520 of the *Complutense*, that six-volume work in several languages which laid the foundation for research into the Bible. The great Cervantes was born in Alcalá in 1547.

125 The plateresque façade of the Colegio de San Ildefonso, the university's principal building, dates from 1543.

126 The cloisters erected by Pedro de la Cotera in 1557 are named "patio trilingue" after the three languages—Latin, Greek and Hebrew—which were taught there.

127-34 TOLEDO, a provincial capital with a population of 34,500, see of the cardinal-primate of the Spanish Church, is situated 1,800 feet above sea-level on a hill within a loop of the River Tajo. The Romans conquered *Toletum*, whose origins are half-legendary, in 192 B.C.; they made it into a colonia and the chief town of Carpetania. Already shortly after the introduction of Christianity important Church Assemblies began to be held here; that of 589 determined the victory of Catholicism over Arianism. As the place of residence of the Gothic kings, Toledo was one of the wealthiest towns in Spain, when, in 712, it fell into Moorish hands. It continued to thrive, thanks primarily to the enterprising Jewish element among its inhabitants. In 1012 the Governor appointed by the Caliphate of Córdoba founded an independent kingdom, wherein Arab-Jewish culture reached a zenith. Alfonso VI of León and Castile captured Toledo in 1085, and made it his capital two years later. The peaceful co-existence of the three denominations and cultures was ended at the close of the fifteenth century by the expulsion of the Jews, the banning of Arabic and the introduction of the Inquisition. At the beginning of the sixteenth century Toledo was at the forefront of the movement of the "Comuneros" against royal despotism; nevertheless, Charles V preferred this to any of the other Castilian towns, and after Philip II had transferred the seat of government to Madrid, Toledo retained the title "imperial y coronada". The Alcázar of Toledo was the scene of one of the most dramatic events of the Civil War: from 22 July until 27 September, 1936, the Nationalist garrison under Colonel Moscardo here withstood the assaults of the Republicans.

127 The PUERTA DEL SOL (Sun Gate) was built at the beginning of the fourteenth century by the Hospitallers in Moorish style.

128 *130* The CATHEDRAL was founded in the time of the Goths by the first bishop, St Eugene, was converted into a mosque by the Arabs and changed back again into a church after the Reconquista. Ferdinand the Holy decided to replace the old building with a new one, as a result of which the mighty Gothic cathedral arose between 1227 and 1493; the west front was added in the sixteenth century, though the 295-feet-high tower on its left side was built between 1380 and 1440 by Rodrigo Alfonso and Álvar Gómez.

129 The MURALLAS DE LA CAVA constitute part of the fortifications by the San Martín bridge.

130 *12B* The SAN MARTÍN BRIDGE (thirteenth and fourteenth centuries), the western approach to the town across the Tajo.

131 SANTA MARÍA LA BLANCA is Toledo's oldest synagogue; it was founded in about 1180, reconstructed in the thirteenth century and converted into a church in 1405. Thirty-two pillars with Moorish arches divide the interior into five aisles.

132-3 EL GRECO'S HOUSE, which the great painter is said to have occupied, the marqués de Vega Inclán had restored and, with its garden, opened to the public as a typical example of a sixteenth-century fashionable private residence. The Cretan Domenico Theotocopuli, called El Greco, came to Toledo in 1577, and worked there until his death in 1614. His creative genius was not confined to painting, for he was also a sculptor, architect, writer and musician.

134 The church of SAN JUAN DE LOS REYES belonged to a monastery which the Catholic Monarchs founded in 1476 to commemorate the victory which was won over the Portuguese near Toledo. The sumptuous plateresque interior ornamentation shows the coat of arms and initials of Ferdinand and Isabella. The royal couple were buried in the church, which was designed by Juan Guas, but their remains were later transferred to Granada.

35-45 MADRID is situated 1,903–2,283 feet above sea-level on the gently undulating, sandy plateau of New Castile. Referred to by its Arabic name, Maǧrīt, for the first time in the tenth century, the place was of little significance in medieval times. Not until the fourteenth century did the kings of Castile begin to hold their courts there; Charles V made the old castle into a royal residence and in 1560 Philip II declared Madrid the capital of the Spanish Empire and its "única corte". Since then, it has steadily grown in importance as state and government have become more centralized. Today the buildings and straight roads of the nineteenth and twentieth centuries give the city its characteristic modern appearance, and it is still rapidly developing. At the turn of the century Madrid, with its 540,000 inhabitants, had outstripped all other Spanish towns; today (counting the suburbs) this number has increased to two million.

135 View of the town from the west, across the valley of the Manzanares. On the left, a sky-scraper; on the right, the extensive royal palace built in the eighteenth and nineteenth centuries to replace the earlier Alcázar.

136 The PRADO Museum (Museo Nacional de Pintura y Escultura) is housed in a classical-style building, erected in 1785, under Charles III, by Juan de Villanueva, as a museum of natural history. The collection, one of the finest in the world, originated in the art treasures owned by Charles V and Philip II. Among their successors, however, there were ardent art-lovers who had court painters such as Velasquez and Goya in their service, and in 1819 Ferdinand VII had all the paintings scattered in various royal palaces brought together under one roof. In front of the colonnade facing the Paseo de Prado (left) stands the Velasquez monument by Marinas (1899).

137 The UNIVERSITY TOWN (Ciudad Universitaria), which lies in the north-west of Madrid and comprises various groups of buildings representing different faculties and institutes, was the scene of violent fighting during the Civil War (1936-9); it has since been rebuilt on generous lines. The buildings shown in the picture belong to the medical faculty. The University of Madrid originated in the sixteenth century as a school, and attained its leading position only in the first half of the nineteenth century when the University of Alcalá de Henares closed down.

138 "EL RETIRO" is a large park first laid out in the fifteenth, extended in the seventeenth and deriving its present appearance from the nineteenth century; in the middle is situated the lake with the equestrian statue of King Alfonso XII (d. 1885) by Mariano Benlliure (1922).

139 View from one of the tall blocks of flats down the Avenida de José Antonio, the former "Gran Via".

140 PLAZA DE ESPAÑA with the Cervantes memorial (1927); in the foreground are bronze statues of Don Quixote and Sancho Panza, in the background a building of twenty-four stories completed in 1952.

141-5 CORRIDA (Bull fight) in the Plaza de Toros in Madrid during commemoration week for the patron saint of the city, San Isidro (May).

141-3 The final stages of the fight: the mounted *picadores* have attacked the bull with their spears and the *banderilleros* have plunged their darts into its back; the *matador*, the leader of the *cuadrilla*, faces the bull alone, with his dagger and crimson cloth (*muleta*); after what is usually an exciting encounter he delivers the death-blow.

144 A team of mules gallops out of the arena with the dead bull.

145 The spectators give the successful *matador* and his team a big ovation as they parade around the arena. Three teams or *cuadrillas*, who each engage in two fights, make up a *corrida*.

146-8 ARANJUEZ on the Tajo, thirty miles south of Madrid. Here in the fourteenth century the Master of the Order of the Knights of Santiago built himself a country estate, which passed to the Spanish crown in 1522. During and after the reign of Charles V it was used by the Court in spring. In 1561 Philip II commissioned Juan Bautista de Toledo and Juan de Herrera, the architects of the Escorial, to build a new palace; following a series of disastrous fires it was rebuilt by Pedro Caro for Philip V in the first half of the eighteenth century. The famous gardens, too, were augmented on a grand scale during that century.

147 The great courtyard of the ROYAL PALACE which is today used as a museum.

148 The CASA DEL LABRADOR ("Countryman's House"), a little castle in the style of the Trianon at Versailles,

was built in about 1800 by Isidro González Velazquez for Charles IV. It stands in the large park on the Tajo (Jardín del Príncipe).

149 CUENCA, provincial capital and see of the bishops of New Castile, stands on a hill above the confluence of the rivers Júcar and Huécar, at the foot of the Serranía de Cuenca, at a height of 3,025–3,355 feet. Built above a ravine are the CASAS COLGADAS (hanging houses). Known since Roman times, it was not until 1177, under Alfonso VIII, that Cuenca was won back from the Moors after a siege lasting nine months.

150 The CIUDAD ENCANTADA, about twenty miles north of Cuenca; its fantastic rock formations are the result of the erosion of Mesozoic chalk deposits.

151 Landscape with olive plantations in New Castile, between Aranjuez and Quintanar.

152 Houses near OCAÑA (Toledo province).

153 MOTA DE CUERVO (Cuenca province), where several potteries produce the characteristic jars of the Mancha district.

154 One of the Mancha windmills, immortalized by Cervantes in his *Don Quixote*. The Mancha (the name probably derives from the Arabic "manǧa", i.e. "plateau") is a plain in New Castile with vast, ocean-like expanses; but rivers have cut wide ravines into the otherwise barren soil, where crops and olives grow.

155 Sheep grazing on the outskirts of CORRAL DE ALMAGUER (Toledo province), a village near Aranjuez on the plateau of New Castile.

156 Women at the well of a village in the MANCHA.

157 The village of LAGARTERA, in the province of Toledo, is well known for its ancient handicrafts: embroidery and filigree work.

158 OROPESA (Toledo province). View from the castle across the fields and olive trees of the New Castilian plain in the direction of Madrid. The castle with its massive fortified towers was built in 1366 for the counts of Frias; the new wing dating from 1402 now houses a parador (inn) run by the Tourist Organization.

159–61 The monastery of SANTA MARÍA DE GUADALUPE, on the southern slope of the Sierra de Guadalupe in Estremadura, was founded by Alfonso IX, after his victory over the Moors of 1340. As a place of pilgrimage it was richly endowed, especially during the reigns of the Catholic Monarchs. Columbus stayed here before his discovery of the island which was named after the Virgen de Guadalupe. From 1389 until 1835 it was occupied by the Hieronymites; in 1908 the Franciscans took over the deserted buildings.
Plate 159 shows the strongly fortified group of monastery buildings which towers above the town.

160 The Gothic church of the monastery, whose façade dominates the main square, was built in 1349–63 and restored in the seventeenth century.

161 In the centre of the cloister court, dating from the fourteenth century, this "fountain-pavilion" was erected in 1405. Built in the "Mudéjar" style, it is one of the best examples of the use made of Moorish forms and their characteristic bricks and ornamentation in religious buildings dedicated to the Christian faith.

162–3 On the road between Navahermosa and Guadalupe, in the Puerto de San Vicente region.

164 Modern iron and concrete bridge carrying the Plasencia-Cáceres road across the Tajo, which flows on into Portugal from here.

165–6 TRUJILLO (Cáceres province), 1,696 feet above sea-level, whose name has been given to more than one town in South America, has to a large extent preserved its ancient character from the time of the conquistadores. The fortifications are still in part those of the Iberian *Turgalium* of pre-Roman times. Pizarro, the conqueror of Peru, was born here in 1475; his equestrian statue in bronze, by the American sculptor C. C. Rumsey, was erected in the PLAZA MAYOR (166) in 1927. At a corner of the same square stands the palace of Pizarro's descendants, the counts de la Conquista. Ornamented with coats of arms (165), it dates from the beginning of the seventeenth century.

167 Well on the barren plateau of Estremadura.

168 CÁCERES, 1,440 feet above sea-level, the old capital of the province of Estremadura, stands on the site of the Roman colonia, *Caesarina Norbensis*, on the road

leading from Mérida to Salamanca. The Arabs settled here in the ninth century. During the battles between Moors and Christians in the twelfth and thirteenth centuries the town changed hands several times; it was again the scene of much fighting during the Civil Wars and those with Portugal.

THE CASA DE LOS GOLFINES, with its characteristic plateresque cornice (late fifteenth century) above fortress-like walls, once housed the Catholic Monarchs; their anagram "fer de fer" appears in relief over the entrance.

169 MÉRIDA (Badajoz province) was founded in 23 B.C. under Augustus; as *Augusta Emerita* it was the capital of Lusitania and one of the principal Roman localities on the peninsula, capable of accommodating a garrison of 90,000 men. A number of existing buildings date from this period, among them the particularly well-preserved theatre, built in 18 B.C. under Agrippa, which held 5,500 spectators; a colonnade was added to the stage under Hadrian.

70-5 SEVILLA (Seville), the fourth largest town in Spain, with a population approaching 400,000, is situated in the fertile Andalusian plain on the lower Guadalquivir which, in ancient times, was called Baetis and was navigable up to this point. "Hispalis", as it was known in early times, was in turn used by the Phoenicians, Greeks and Carthaginians as a trading centre; it was conquered by Caesar in 45 B.C., and occupied by the Vandals, the Visigoths and the Moors in 411, 441 and 712 respectively. After the decline of Córdoba in the eleventh century, Seville became the leading city in Mohammedan Spain and flourished both economically and culturally, in particular under the Almohads (after 1146). It was occupied by Ferdinand III in 1248, when Christianity was enforced as the official religion; after the discovery of America the monopoly of oversea trade brought it renewed prosperity. Alfonso X (the Wise), who sometimes made Seville his place of residence in the second half of the thirteenth century, bestowed on the city, in recognition of its loyalty, the following motto: "Muy noble, muy leal, muy heroica e invencible" (Most noble, most loyal, most heroic and invincible.)

70-3 Construction of the ALCÁZAR, seat of the Almohad princes, was continued on a grand scale even in Christian times, especially under the Castilian king, Peter I (the Cruel). It was carried out by converted Moors in the style of the refined, courtly art of the Mohammedans; additional building and restoration work was undertaken for the wedding of Charles V in 1526.

170 Shows the view from the Alcázar towards the Cathedral.

171-2 The gardens of the Alcázar. With their fountains and pavilions and—in May-time—a profusion of blossom, they are a unique example of the blending of Oriental and Occidental enchantment.

173 View from the PATIO DE LAS MUÑECAS (Dolls' Courtyard) through the SALON DE EMBAJADORES (Ambassadors' Hall), a masterpiece in the "Mudéjar" style from the time of Peter I, towards the rooms of María de Padilla.

174 The CATHEDRAL was built in the fifteenth century on the site of the earlier mosque. It incorporated the great twelfth-century minaret which was crowned with a belfry in the sixteenth century.

175 The so-called CASA DE PILATOS, now in the possession of the Count of Medinaceli, was built in the fifteenth and sixteenth centuries for Pedro Henríquez and his son, the first marquis of Tarifa. The courtyard, with its azulejos (cf. colour plate I) and stucco ornamentation, is one of the finest examples of the "Mudéjar" style. The corner-statue of Minerva comes from the ruins of the Roman colonia *Itálica* in what is now the suburbs of Seville.

176 ANDALUSIAN WOMAN in special costume with castanets, dancing the "Sevillana". Among the wealth of Spanish folk music, with its great regional variety of song and dance, it is the Andalusian tunes and rhythms with their Oriental beat which, more than any other, have influenced and fascinated musicians in other countries.

177 RONDA, a town of some 30,000 inhabitants, 2,460 feet above sea-level (Málaga province), lies on the edge of a rocky plateau in the Serrania de Ronda which, for a distance of over half a mile, drops some 660 feet almost vertically to the plain. It was this dominating situation which enabled the Moorish kings of Granada to use the place as a border fortress from 1097 until 1485. The two halves of the town are connected by a bridge

which spans the deep gorge of the Guadiaro. To the left of our photograph can be seen the round Plaza de Toros (bull-fighting arena), so noticeable a feature of Spanish towns, when viewed from the air.

(THIS IS THE OLDIEST BULL RING)

178-9 ANTEQUERA (Malaga province), the Roman *Anticaria*, situated 1,680 feet above sea-level in a fertile valley by the Sierra de Torcales, was already settled in prehistoric times. Plate 179 shows a typical Andalusian street scene.

180 ALDEA DE LA QUINTANA (Córdoba province), in Andalusia, is little more than a collection of straw-thatched cottages on a height between Seville and Córdoba.

181 LOJA (Granada province), an Andalusian town on the Río Genil.

182 At the summit of the Cabeza (a 2,059-feet-high mountain), in the highlands of the province of Jaén, stands the church of NUESTRA SEÑORA DE LA CABEZA (or VIRGEN DE LA CABEZA). This goal of a famous pilgrimage (romería) is cared for by the Trinitarian monks. The wooden statue of the Virgin was, according to legend, brought to Spain by St Luke; during Moorish rule it was hidden in the mountains where, in the thirteenth century, it was found by a shepherd in miraculous circumstances.

183 MÁLAGA, in Andalusia, with a population of 300,000, is one of the foremost Spanish ports and famous for marketing the sweet wine which thrives particularly well in this region. "Malaka" or "Malacha" was, next to Gades, the most important Tyrian colony in Spain and as early as the first century A.D. became a bishop's see. Between 711 and 1487 it was under Moorish rule, during which time this erstwhile seat of a small, independent kingdom became one of their mightiest fortresses. Even after its conquest, the Moorish element still predominated under the reign of Catholic Monarchs. After the Declaration of the Republic in 1931 and during the Civil War (1936) the churches and monasteries of the town suffered much damage. The aerial photograph shows, in the right foreground, the Alcazaba (fortress), constructed mainly in the ninth century on ancient foundations; a wall joins it to the CASTILLO DE GIBRALFARO. To the right are harbour installations and the Plaza de Toros.

184 JAÉN, a provincial capital with a population of over 50,000, is situated 1,883 feet above sea-level, and was the ancient *Aurgi*. Fortified by Hasdrubal, and won back from Carthage by the Scipios, it became prominent under the Romans because of the silver mines of the district. The Arabs here founded a small kingdom of their own, "ǵaiyán" (Jaén), which was first subject to the caliphs of Córdoba, then to the kings of Granada. After its conquest by Ferdinand III in 1246, until the fall of Granada in 1492, Jaén was an outpost of the Reconquista. The town lies at the foot of the hill on which the Moorish fortress stands; the cathedral has large twin towers and a Baroque façade.

185 In a fertile plain between Andújar and Córdoba, through which the Guadalquivir flows, this stone ROMAN BRIDGE spanning the tributary Salado de Porcuna recalls the ancient "Via Augusta".

186-91 CÓRDOBA, today a provincial capital of about 150,000 inhabitants, was the first Roman colonia in Spain and flourished as principal locality of the province of Hispania ulterior. Hosius, its bishop, was president of the first council of Nicæa in 345. After the Arab invasion of 715, and especially during the early part of the great dynasty of the Omayyads who in 756 set up an independent caliphate, Córdoba became one of the most splendid capitals in the Mohammedan world, whose renown as a seat of art and learning, especially mathematics, extended as far as Christian Europe. In the ninth and tenth centuries the town is said to have had a population of 300,000, 300 mosques and a number of magnificent palaces. Its decline was due to the arrival of the Berbers in 1010 and the rivalry of various dynasties; Ferdinand III had no difficulty in occupying it in 1236.

186 View of the so-called ROMAN BRIDGE from the left bank of the Guadalquivir. Dating mainly from Moorish times and frequently restored in the course of the centuries, it is nearly 800 feet long and has sixteen arches; beyond, the cathedral rises above the Old Town.

187 The little PLAZA DEL POTRO with the statue of St Raphael in the foreground and, behind it, the well with the figure of a foal (potro). Cervantes, who mentions the square in his *Don Quixote*, is said to have been a lodger in one of the houses.

216

188 A typical alley in the Old Town.

189 A herd of goats reclining by the Moorish bridge-fortress or CALAHORRA on the south bank of the Guadalquivir. The fortress was restored in the fourteenth century.

190-1 Abdurrahman I, having dismantled the church erected by the Goths above a temple of Janus, and compensated the Christians, in 785 started work on the "Great Mosque" which was to surpass all others in splendour. When it was completed its only rival for size was the Ka'ba at Mecca. On the advent of Christianity only a few initial modifications, such as the inclusion of chapels and altars, were made. In the sixteenth century, however, in spite of strenuous opposition from the municipal authorities who wished to preserve their most beautiful architectural monument, a royal decree authorized the incorporation of a choir gallery which entailed extensive alterations. Today the cathedral or "La Mezquita" still dominates the town. The east front (190) retains a large amount of Moorish relief ornamentation. The interior (191) is a forest of about 850 pillars made of granite and precious marble from all over the world, some of it even from ancient temples. The two tiers of arches are made of alternating bands of white stone and red brick.

192-9 GRANADA, capital of the province and an archbishop's see, with a population of over 150,000, is situated 2,049 feet above sea-level in the north-western foothills of the Sierra Nevada, above a wide, fertile plain (Vega). We hear of it already in the fifth century B.C. as the Iberian "Iliberris"; the Arabs gave it the name of "Garnāta" in the eighth century, but it began to attain its position as the leading Moorish centre in Spain only in the eleventh century, after the extinction of the Omayyad dynasty. After the fall of Córdoba in 1236, Granada remained for a further two and a half centuries the seat of an Islamic empire on the Spanish Mediterranean coast, where under the Nasride dynasty (after 1241) commerce and culture flourished. As early as 1350 Granada is said to have had a population of 200,000, which in the fifteenth century, when fifty academies and seventy libraries were at their disposal, had risen to 500,000. Internal disputes as to who should occupy the throne favoured the Catholic Monarchs' assault on this last bulwark of the Moors, and in January 1492, Ferdinand and Isabella entered the town in whose cathedral they were later to be laid to rest. During the reign of Philip II Granada and the surrounding districts suffered badly under the bloody suppression of Christians of Moorish origin.

192 View of the hill of "Cerro del Sol" and the ALHAMBRA from the north-west. This was the citadel of the Moorish rulers and owes its name (al-Hamrā, "the Red") to the reddish stone of which it is built.

193 View from the ALCAZABA (fortress), the oldest, eastern part of the Alhambra, towards the Sierra Nevada.

194 The palace buildings of the ALCÁZAR, the actual royal residence inside the Alhambra, date mainly from the fourteenth century. The unbelievable splendour of this monument to a highly refined and distinguished culture remained untouched by the Catholic Monarchs; but under Charles V alterations were carried out to make room for a new palace. In the eighteenth century the place was completely neglected, but from 1830 onwards the significance of this unique building and the need to restore it in a worthy manner were once more appreciated. The view towards the TORRE DE COMARES obtained from the PATIO DE LOS ARRAYANES (Courtyard of Myrtles), also called PATIO DE LA ALBERCA (Courtyard of the Pool), emphasizes the contrast between the noble architecture of the interior and the sober strength of the fortified outer walls.

195 The MIRADOR DE DARAXA, in which Islamic ornamental art is seen at its finest. No representations of living objects, but Arabic calligraphic symbols are employed in its abstract design.

196 The SALA DE LAS DOS HERMANAS (Hall of the Two Sisters) with its splendid stalactite cupola.

197-8 The LION COURTYARD is surrounded by arcades made up of 128 slender, white marble columns. In the centre stands the fountain, supported by twelve lions.

199 To the east of Alhambra, on a hill just overlooking it, the royal summer palace GENERALIFE, built in the fourteenth century, stands amid terraced gardens.

200 View of the mountainous hinterland of the Mediterranean coast, as seen from the road between Granada and Motril.

201 The Mediterranean coast between Motril and Almería where orchards nestle between the bare mountain ridges.

202-3 ALMERÍA, capital of the province of that name, with 80,000 inhabitants, is a Mediterranean port which ships mainly fruits and esparto. It was originally a Phoenician settlement; its Arab name means "Mountain Peace". In the eleventh century in particular Almería, seat of a Moorish kingdom which at times maintained its independence, was one of the most flourishing cities in the peninsula; its Court patronized poets and men of letters. After the first Christian occupation in 1147 its harbour was several times the subject of disputes between the Mediterranean powers. In the last century the town suffered as a result of the Civil Wars. Both photographs are taken from the platform of the fortress-like cathedral tower; the first shows the view towards the harbour, the other the ALCAZABA, rising beyond the flat roofs of the town. This hill fortress was built in the tenth century by the caliph, Abdurrahman III, and enlarged by the local rulers in the following century.

204-5 Two views, taken between Almería and Sorbas, of the countryside near Huércal-Overa. The Huertas, with their palms and orange trees, lie like oases in the river valleys between the bare, desert-like mountain ridges.

206 ORIHUELA (Alicante province), the ancient Orcelis which the Arabs called Uriyūla, forms the centre of a richly cultivated Huerta, irrigated by canals.

207 MURCIA, provincial capital with a population of 60,000, called Mursiya by the Arabs, was an independent kingdom for a short time during the thirteenth century, before its annexation by Castile. Under Alfonso X (the Wise), Catalans, Aragonese and Provençals were settled here. Work on the cathedral which replaced the mosque was begun in 1394 and continued until the sixteenth century; the plateresque octagonal chapel DE LOS VÉLEZ, to the east of the main building, was erected at the end of the fifteenth century.

208 The PEÑÓN DE IFACH (Alicante province), an extinct volcano 984 feet high, on the headland of Calpe.

209 Promenade along the harbour at ALICANTE, provincial capital with 100,000 inhabitants. Despite its ancient origins, there is a modern air about this Mediterranean town, with its beautiful climate.

210 The PALM FOREST OF ELCHE (Alicante province), irrigated by canals, resembles a North African oasis; the exceptionally mild climate produces a plentiful crop of dates.

211,213 VALENCIA, third largest city of Spain, with a population of 500,000, is the capital of one of the country's most fertile provinces. It was ruled in turn by Greeks, Carthaginians, Romans, Goths (413-714) and Moors; in 1094 it was conquered by the Cid and ruled by him until his death five years later. In 1101 the Moors reconquered the town and in 1146 set up an independent kingdom there, but this became subject to Alfonso II of Aragon, and in 1238 was wholly annexed by James I (the Conqueror). Towards the end of the fifteenth century Valencia was allotted a Castilian vice-regent, and in 1500 a university was founded, the products of whose printing presses are among the earliest and most valuable in Spain. At the beginning of the seventeenth century, the expulsion of the industrious Christian Moors proved an economic setback for the city. In the nineteenth century Valencia played a leading role in the various revolutionary movements, and again between 1932 and 1936 many of its monasteries and churches were wrecked; in 1939, towards the end of the Civil War, it was the last seat of the Republican government.

211 The LONJA DE LA SEDA (Silk Exchange) was built 1483-98 by Pedro Compte in Late Gothic style. The right half of the building, shown here, contains the old exchange hall of the silk merchants.

213 The TORRES DE SARRANOS form part of the walls of the medieval town, evidence of which still remains in many of the modern streets. The north-east gate was erected under James I of Aragon in 1238, and the two towers were added 1592-8 by Pedro Compte.

212 SAGUNTO (Valencia province), called Murviedro (from "muro vetero") until 1877, is surmounted by the Castillo, built on ancient ruins. The Celtiberian town was conquered by Hannibal in 219 B.C. when the heroic population destroyed itself and its property to avoid falling into the enemy's hands. Under the Romans *Saguntum* became an important town; among other architectural remains there is a theatre dating from this period.

214 PEÑÍSCOLA (province of Castillón de la Plana), a rocky promontory jutting into the Mediterranean, was in antiquity occupied by Iberians, Phoenicians, Greeks, Carthaginians and Romans. After the conquest of 1234 James I handed it over to the Templars, who built a new fortress on it. The anti-pope Benedict XIII (Peter de Luna), deposed at the Council of Constance, retired here in 1414 and persisted with his claims until the time of his death in 1423.

215 A herd of goats in the Sagunto district.

216-17 TARRAGONA, now a provincial capital with nearly 40,000 inhabitants, was one of the most flourishing seaports in the Roman Empire. An Iberian fortified town, it was captured by the Romans in 218 B.C. during the second Punic war and made into one of their most important bases in Hispania. In 26 B.C. Augustus spent the winter here and made *Tarraco* the capital of Hispania Citerior. Its climate and wine were celebrated by Martial and Pliny. Tradition has it that St Paul himself converted the place to Christianity; it was made an archiepiscopal see in the fifth century and today the Archbishop of Tarragona still shares with the Archbishop of Toledo the title of Spanish Primate. Between the twelfth and fourteenth centuries altogether twenty-three councils were held here. In the course of its eventful history the town was sacked several times: by the Visigoths, the Moors, and, in more modern times, the British (1705) and the French (1811). In the twelfth century it was under Norman occupation and in the thirteenth finally became part of Catalonia. The discovery of America, which benefited many other ports, deprived Tarragona of much of its earlier importance.

216 The Gothic façade of the CATHEDRAL, built 1120-1331, is adorned with statues of apostles and prophets. The early part of the doorway is by Bartolomeo the Norman (1278), the later figures are by Jaime Castais of Saragossa (1475).

217 The ROMAN WALLS were built on top of solid blocks of the old *murallas ciclopeas* (cyclopean walls).

218-19 The monastery of SANTA MARÍA DE POBLET (Tarragona province) was founded in 1153 by Ramón Berenguer, Count of Barcelona and King of Aragon, and inhabited by the monks of Fontfroide, near Narbonne. The huge Cistercian abbey enjoyed also the special patronage of Ramón's descendants; Peter IV had a mausoleum built for them in the monastic church in 1387 where, among other kings of Aragon, James I lies buried. During the Civil War of 1835 the buildings were deserted, but have once more been occupied by monks since 1940.

218 The cloisters, with their covered well in the centre, date from the middle of the thirteenth century.

219 The retable, with its wealth of carved statues, which Damián Forment produced for the Emperor Charles V in 1529 to adorn the twelfth-century monastic church built under Alfonso II of Aragon.

220 Landscape near Igualada (Barcelona province) showing how the Río Noya has hollowed its deep course through the mountain plateau.

221 LÉRIDA, capital of the province of that name, with 40,000 inhabitants. The Roman *Ilerda*, where Caesar defeated Pompey in 49 B.C., was captured from the Moors in 1149 by Ramón Berenguer, Count of Barcelona. This strongly fortified place was frequently disputed in battle by the Spanish and French; it successfully withstood an attack by the Condé in the seventeenth century, but was captured by the Duke of Orleans in 1707 and by Suchet in 1810. During the Civil War (1936) its religious buildings were damaged. View of the town across the Río Segre, with the hill fortress on which rises the old cathedral (Cathedral Vieja or Seo Antigua). This fine thirteenth-century building stood empty for a long time; it was used as a barracks in the eighteenth century and is now being restored.

222 COLL DE NARGÓ, valley of the Río Segre between Seo de Urgel and Lérida.

223-4 RIPOLL (Gerona province), 2,234 feet up in the Pyrenees, was originally built around the monastery of SANTA MARÍA, which was founded in the sixth century, destroyed by Arabs and rebuilt after 888. The cloisters and the monastic church are among the greatest monuments of Romanesque art in Catalonia; the two-storied cloisters (223) date from the twelfth and fourteenth centuries, the elaborate "Triumphal Arch of Christendom" (224) on the west front, which is unique of its kind, was built during the first half of the twelfth century.

225 VICH (Barcelona province), the Roman *Ausa*, at the foot of the Pyrenees, was an archiepiscopal see under the Visigoths; the Arabs destroyed it in 713 and it was rebuilt as a fortress by the Franks in 798. The Romanesque lower story of the cloisters near the eleventh-century cathedral dates from the twelfth century, the upper story, with its Late Gothic arches and delicate tracery, from the fifteenth century.

226 The valley of the RÍO TER between Ripoll and Vich, in the Catalonian Pyrenees.

227 The little Romanesque church of SANTA COLOMA in the state of Andorra which is under the joint suzerainty of the French State (a legacy from the Count of Foix) and the Spanish Bishop of Urgel.

228 SEO DE URGEL (Lérida province), a little town 2,296 feet up in the Pyrenees, has been an episcopal see since the sixth century. The picture shows the east front (partially built over) of the twelfth-century Romanesque cathedral, "La Seu".

229-31 MONTSERRAT (meaning "Blessed Mountain"?) or ✕ "Montsagrat" ("Holy Mountain"), 4,101 feet high with fantastic rock formations, stands almost isolated from the remainder of the Catalonian range. The Benedictine abbey founded in 880, about half-way up the mountain, contains the miraculous image of "Nuestra Señora de Montserrat, Patrona de Cataluña" and is much visited by pilgrims. St Ignatius of Loyola laid his sword on the altar of the Virgin and dedicated his new life to her.

229 The south face of Montserrat with the village of MONISTROL on the Río Llobregat.

230 The monastic building (2,379 feet up) with the church put up under Philip II (1565-92), much altered since. The Romanesque apse was added in 1880.

231 One of the many rocky peaks of Montserrat.

232 SITGES (Barcelona province,) an old town, has been a popular seaside resort since the end of the last century, thanks to its lovely beach. It is a particular favourite with the inhabitants of Barcelona, which is only about twenty-eight miles away.

233 Landscape near Pineda in the mountainous hinterland of the Costa Brava with its many pine forests.

234 SAN POL DE MAR (Barcelona province), one of the fishing villages of the "Marina", between Barcelona and the French border.

235-7 BARCELONA, the old capital of Catalonia, is said to have been founded by the Phocæans. Its old name, "Barcino", is of Iberian or Ligurian origin. It was occupied by the Carthaginians after their invasion of 237 B.C. Under the Romans (after 201 B.C.) the sea-port gained yet more in importance; in 343 its bishopric was established. The Arabs were able to hold Barcelona for only a brief century; at the beginning of the ninth century it was occupied by Charlemagne's son Louis, who made it principal locality in the Spanish March. From 874 until the union with Aragon in 1137 it maintained its independence under the rulership of the Counts of Barcelona, and during this period Catalan culture reached a peak. In the late Middle Ages Barcelona was one of the most important Mediterranean centres of commerce and its maritime laws were adopted by the whole of Europe. In the seventeenth century the King of France supported Barcelona's bid for autonomy and became its temporary sovereign. Political unrest in the nineteenth century did not prevent the city from achieving renewed economic eminence, and an ample, modern town with a large, extremely industrious population grew around the old Gothic quarter ("Barrio gótico").

235 View through one of the alleys in the Barrio gótico towards the little PLAZA DEL REY in the middle of the old royal palace with its tower of 1557 (called "Mirador de Mar" or "del Rey Martín").

236 The government building (Palacio de la generalidad), formerly "Audiencia", a Gothic building of the fifteenth century. Around the upper story of the courtyard runs a gallery as found in cloisters.

237 The old harbour of Barcelona. A faithful reconstruction of the "Santa María" commemorates Christopher Columbus's epoch-making voyage which made Spain the centre of a world-wide empire.

✕ MORE PROBABLY 'SERRATED' OR SAW TOOTHED MOUNTAIN.

ACKNOWLEDGMENTS

Acknowledgment is made to the following for kindly supplying photographs to supplement the author's own material: Frl. Relang, Munich (Plate 176), Snr. Pietzsch, Madrid (Plate 182), Labor, Barcelona (Plates 21, 149, photo, Mas; 150, photo Garrabella, Zaragoza; 177 and 183).

The author also wishes to thank Professor Arnald Steiger for his valuable help in connection with the Notes.

INDEX

Alcalá de Henares . 125–126
Aldea de la Quintana . 180
Alicante . . . 209
Almería . . 202–203
Alsasua . . . 6
Andorra . . . 227
Antequera . . 178–179
Aragón, Río . . 12, 18
Aranda de Duero . 74
Aranjuez . . 146–147
Arcos, Los . . . 8
Arga, Río . . . 11
Arguis, Puerto de . 17
Arguis Dam . . 16
Asturian Farm . 43
Ávila . . . 104–110
Azpeitia . . . 7

Barcelona . . 235–237
Béjar . . . 64
Bermeo . . . 29
Bilbao . . . 32
Burgos . . . 35–41

Cabeza, Nuestra Señora de la 182
Cáceres . . . 168
Calatayud . . 23
Campos Carpetanos . 95
Cantabrian Coast . 1–2, 29
Castile Canal . . 82
Ciudad Encantada . 150
Coca . . . 91–93
Coll de Nargó . . 222
Coloma, Santa . . 227
Córdoba . . 186–191
Corral de Almaguer . 155
Coruña, La . . 46–48
Cuenca . . . 149

Dueñas . . . 78
Duero . . . 73

Ebro . . . 21
Elche . . . 210

El Paular . . . 111
Escó . . . 12
Escorial . . 117–120
Estella . . . 9–10

Gerona . . . VII
Granada . . 192–199, 111
Granja, La . . 115–116
Guadalajara . . 124
Guadalquivir . . 186
Guadalupe . . 159–161
Guadarrama, Sierra de
                  103, 113–114
Guernica, Bay of . . 28

Huesca . . 19–20

Ifach, Peñón de . . 208
Igualada . . . 220

Jaca . . . 14–15
Jaén . . . 184

La Coruña . . 46–48
Lagartera . . 157
La Granja . . 115–116
León . . . 58–62
Lérida . . . 221
Lizarza . . . 5
Llanes . . . 44
Llobregat, Río . . 229
Loja . . . 181
Los Arcos . . . 8
Los Monegros . . 22
Loyola . . . 7
Lugo . . . 54
Lumbier . . . 13

Madrid . . 135–145
Málaga . . . 183
Mancha . . 154–156
Manzanares el Real . 112

Medina del Campo . . 75
Medinaceli . . . 121
Mérida . . . 169
Mondoñedo . . 45
Monegros, Los . . 22
Monistrol . . . 229
Montserrat . . 229–231
Mota de Cuervo . . 153
Muela, de la, Meseta . VIII
Murcia . . . 207

Navacerrada Pass . 113–114
Nevada, Sierra . . 193
Nuestra Señora de la Cabeza 182

Ocaña . . . 152
Ondarroa . . . 4
Orio . . . 3
Orihuela . . . 206
Oropesa . . . 158
Oruña Pass . . 30
Oviedo . . . 42

Pamplona . . . 11
Pancorbo . . . 27
Paular, El . . . 111
Peñafiel . . . 77
Peñiscola . . . 214
Peñón de Ifach . . 208
Piedrafita Pass . . 56
Pineda . . . 233
Poblet . . 218–219
Ponferrada . . 55

Rioja, la . . . 24
Ripoll . . 223–224
Ronda . . . 177
Rudrón, Río . . 31

Sagunto . . . 212
Salamanca . . 65–72, VI
San Ildefonso . . 115–116

San Ignacio de Loyola . 7
San Pol de Mar . . 234
San Sebastián . . . IV
Santa Coloma . . 227
Santiago de Compostela 49–53
Santillana del Mar . 33–34
Saragossa: *see* Zaragoza
Segovia . . . 97–102
Seo de Urgel . . . 228
Sevilla . . . 170–175, I
Sigüenza . . 122–123

Sitges 232

Tajo, Río . . 130, 164, II
Tarragona . . 216–217
Ter, Río . . . 226
Toledo . . . 127–134, II
Tordesillas . . . 76
Tormes, Río . . 68, VI
Trujillo . . . 165–166
Turégano . . . 81

Urgel, Seo de . . 228

Valencia . . 211, 213
Valladolid . . 83–90, V
Venta de Baños . 79–80
Vich 225
Vitoria . . . 25–26

Zamora 63
Zaragoza . . . 21